A Patch
in the
Forest

A Patch in the Forest

by
Elizabeth West
with drawings by
Bernard Kear

Logaston Press

LOGASTON PRESS
Little Logaston Woonton Almeley
Herefordshire HR3 6QH

First published by Logaston Press 2001
Copyright (text) © Elizabeth West 2001
Copyright (drawings) © Bernard Kear 2001

ISBN 1 873827 72 5

Set in Times by Logaston Press
and printed in Great Britain by
Bell & Bain Ltd., Glasgow

Contents

I prayed for: a plot of land, not so very large, containing a garden; and near the homestead a spring of fresh water, and a bit of woodland to complete it.

Horace, 65-8 B.C.

Well, we knew that we were unlikely to find that spring of fresh water. There can't be much pure, uncontaminated, unpolluted, clean, drinkable water available now. Most of us have to make do (fingers crossed) with what comes out of the tap. But, even 2,000 years after Horace's prayer we could perhaps find that plot of land with its garden, homestead and

bit of woodland ...

CHAPTER 1

The Search

We found this house by accident, having been misdirected (or having misunderstood directions) to another place. It is very easy to get lost in the Forest of Dean. Alan blames the underlying iron-bearing rock which he claims affects his 'internal compass'—when the map indicates that one should clearly turn in a certain direction he often has an irresistible compulsion to go the other way. We had been driving around a network of lanes trying to follow the Agent's direction to 'Cosy Cot' which was for sale. Now Forest of Dean lanes are surely unique. They twist downwards through wet patches, climb upwards between high hedges, meander through the grassy remains of old mine workings, and often come to a dead end for no apparent reason. Inviting side lanes, usually unsignposted, can lead to a brooding Forestry Commission woodland, a charming hamlet or a second-hand tyre depot. We decided to stop in the next village that had a pub and ask for help. Over our glasses of beer at the Pick and Shovel we consulted the landlady and found her to be most obliging. She not only gave us precise directions to 'Cosy Cot' but also insisted upon telling us about a cottage *she* had for sale. It was called 'The Laurels' and was in the middle of some woods a couple of miles away.

We didn't like 'Cosy Cot'. It was at the bottom of a valley and had three very close neighbours, all of whom were in a slightly elevated position and were able to stare without interruption into 'Cosy Cot's' garden. So we decided we might as well go and have a look at 'The Laurels'. A few miles further on we turned off the road and followed a track through the forest until we came to a stop where a Forestry Commission gate barred the way. So we left the car and started

1

walking. According to Alan the instructions were to keep on turning left. It was a warm October afternoon and the sunshine was flickering through the trees. Meadow brown and speckled wood butterflies were dancing over the grasses and a wren chattered crossly at us from the top of a gorse bush at the side of the track. We found a large patch of bramble bushes and stopped to pick some blackberries, and a laden rowan tree which we admired but left alone. We found sweet chestnuts littering the path, a large patch of shaggy inkcap fungi and a solitary horse mushroom. But we couldn't find 'The Laurels'. Nor, when we came to look for it, could we find the path back to the car. It was Alan's fault of course. I reminded him that he was old and deaf and I suggested that he had probably misheard the directions. He said that I was old and daft and had probably not *understood* the directions. I must admit I hadn't been listening properly to the pub land-lady, for I was much too busy trying to remember the directions to 'Cosy Cot' to concentrate on what she was saying about 'The Laurels'. In the event, by making a masterful decision to rely upon his sense of direction and ignore all pathways, Alan led us through shoulder-high bracken, across wet ditches and under low-hanging boughs and we finally got out onto the track again just a few yards away from the car. His 'internal compass' was obviously learning to cope with the underlying metallic rock.

We drove back along the track and were just about to turn into the road when Alan stopped because he saw, emerging from a cottage, a friendly looking chap who might be able to direct us to 'The Laurels'. I didn't want him to bother. I was bad-tempered and fed up with driving around narrow lanes and crawling through dense woods, moreover I had wet feet. I just wanted to go home and have a cup of tea. But the car was turned around, and back we went along the track and parked in the same place as before. But now we were following instructions to keep on turning right, and we soon found 'The Laurels'. It was an interesting looking cottage but it was too small and had a tiny garden. This wouldn't do at all; we wanted plenty of space. So that was that. We could now go home.

But during our to-ing and fro-ing I had noticed a house with a For Sale board in the front garden. It was a gable-ended brick built house standing well back from the track. It had a chimney pot on each gable, a square porch on the front and looked as though it had prob-ably been built in the 1950s. It appeared totally without charm. On passing it for the fourth time it began to dawn on me that I had seen that before somewhere, and I was reasonably sure that an Agent had sent us details of the place. I had taken one glance at the photocopied picture of that dreary frontage and thrown the details away. However, although the house itself was unappealing, the situation was excellent. When we got home I scrabbled around in the wastepaper basket and retrieved the Agent's particulars: there was the photograph—a badly photocopied full frontal showing four windows and a square porch stuck on the front. My reaction when I had first seen that photograph, and before throwing it away, was 'No thank you'. But now that I had seen its situation and, taking all things into consideration, my reasoned and objective reaction was—'No thank you'.

But we bought the house and we still live there.

I think perhaps I had better back-track and explain a few things. During the early years of our married life we lived in a remote, primitive moorland cottage 1,000ft. above sea level in North Wales. We had no mains services. We lit the cottage by paraffin lamp and candle (and occasional home-made electricity from a simple windcharger) and we collected our water in buckets from a spring. We grew trees, shrubs, flowers, vegetables and soft fruits. We had nine acres of rough hillside with views over Snowdonia, but we didn't have any settled way of earning a living. We had made a garden in the wilderness, but after thirteen years we were obliged to sell our moorland home and return to the city. This was to be a temporary move. We promised ourselves that one day, as soon as we were entitled to a state old-age pension, we would find another patch of land in a wild and lonely place and make another garden.

Now that the time to make our plans had arrived we found that the passing years had modified our ideas. With old age ahead we didn't want our patch to be too wild and lonely, nor did we reckon on coping with more than about an acre of land. A place on the outskirts of a village or hamlet would be ideal—preferably on a no-through road and within a half-mile walk of a post office and bus service. Where should we look? We decided not to return to Wales as we wanted to end our days in a locality where our West Country accents would not be out of place, so we limited our search to Devon, Somerset, Wiltshire, Gloucestershire, Herefordshire and Shropshire.

Over the next eighteen months we spent most weekends driving around the countryside peering into other people's houses (which we didn't enjoy doing) and putting up with people coming to peer into ours (which we enjoyed even less). We learned quite a bit about Estate Agents during this period—which was the end of the 1980s when house prices were at their peak and just beginning to tumble. New Estate Agents—many owned by Banks and Building Societies— had opened and in our experience these offices were staffed by bright young people who had plenty of enthusiasm but very little knowledge. The response to our detailed letter of enquiry would be an A4-sized envelope stuffed full of houses, flats, farms (even workshops) very few of which resembled the place we had told them we were looking for. We got the impression that though our requirements had been punched into a computer, in fact every property they had outstanding on their books had been pulled out and sent to us. A fortnight later we would receive another A4-sized envelope containing another sheaf of property descriptions (including some they had sent previously) together with a jolly little note from Kevin (or Mandy or Julian) offering their assistance. About a month later we would receive a duplicated letter to say that they assumed we were no longer looking for a property and they were therefore removing us from their books. And that was the last we heard from Kevin (or Mandy or Julian).

We had more success with personal visits to old established Estate Agents in country market towns. Our visits were always on Sunday mornings and we usually found such offices staffed by middle aged ladies who had been doing the job for many years and, in some cases, had personal knowledge of the property up for sale. Once we found such an Agent we pestered them every week. But no matter how efficient or obliging the counter staff were, we found that the printed details handed out by Estate Agents all used the same sort of language.

After a while we learnt to interpret it. For example: *In need of modernisation* (Falling down); *Subject of extensive refurbishment but still having further scope to extend or improve* (Someone's had a go at it but it's still falling down); *There are new window frames available and plans passed for an attractive extension* (Someone's so fed up with the whole damn place he can't be bothered to do any more); *The property has a stream forming the boundary to one side* (A field ditch which may or may not flood the garden, depending upon the vigilance of the farmer, whose ditch it is); *Gardens largely laid to lawn* (Rough grass that someone has just cut for the benefit of the Agent's photographer);

Useful paddock area (Rough grass that no-one has bothered to cut); *An interesting wild area, left to grow naturally* (A shambles of nettles, thistles, docks, bramble and elder—probably concealing an abandoned refrigerator and old motor bike parts).

Strip lighting was often called *flourescent* (sic), windows were referred to as *aspects* (*patterned aspect over radiator in hall* had us puzzled on one occasion) and if there wasn't much to say about a tiny place the Agent would comment on TV aerial points, under-stair cupboards and take a long paragraph to describe any tatty corrugated-iron lean-to as *a useful store for fuel, garden implements or freezer etc.* We never found out what *inset eyeball spotlights* were (but they sounded rather painful) and if the details mentioned *shared septic tank* or *piped water supply from spring in adjoining field*, we were put off immediately.

Sometimes an Agent's photograph of a rural outlook and woodland garden had us fooled. We once drove to mid-Herefordshire to look at a cottage that appeared to have everything we wanted—stone built, slate roofed, plenty of outbuildings, a Rayburn cooker in the kitchen and a large well-stocked garden. What the photograph didn't show was the huge corrugated iron and brick Farmers' Co-operative grain drying unit that stood beside the garden. It was so close the photographer must have been leaning against it to take his picture.

When a cottage was unoccupied and the key had to be collected from the Agent we were often faced with the sad evidence of someone who had started a renovation job with enthusiasm but had given up in despair. *Footpath approach through woodland* may sound idyllic to someone wanting peace and solitude, but the reality of humping all building materials, fuel and everyday shopping along a muddy and overgrown track must have soured many a hopeful young couple. We once found what one such couple had left behind— looping electric cables from cottage to outbuildings (for the washing machine?), recently decorated walls over which the mould was spreading, 'tide marks' around the back of the house where flood water had lapped, children's toys and broken tools in a shed which looked new but which had not been erected properly, and jackdaws nesting inside a broken chimney pot over a crumbling stack that no-one had got around to repairing.

When primitive and inconveniently situated cottages with large gardens came onto the market they were usually auctioned—especially if the last resident had been an elderly person who had recently died. Although we didn't have the courage to bid at such auctions we sometimes went to look at the property, and we once met the Agent's representative at a tiny cottage in Somerset that was being auctioned with an acre of garden. A mile from the village and with a rough track approach, it overlooked typical rolling English countryside with small hedged fields and distant views of the Mendip Hills. The Agent's representative was a smartly-dressed young lady who unlocked the cottage door with a large key (and some difficulty), shoved it open and stood back to allow us to enter. No-one had bothered to remove the possessions of the old man who had died there. His grubby armchair stood before the fireplace; a threadbare mat lay on the floor and a poker and shovel lay in the hearth. The chimney opening had been fitted with a Yorkseal Combination Grate and I could imagine the cheerful evenings the old man had enjoyed sitting in front of his fire with the kettle singing on the hob and his dog on the mat. (I knew he had a dog because on the front door and doorpost at little-dog height were the greasy marks of an animal that had been accustomed to pushing its way into the house.) We were interested to see that grate because it was the first one we had come across. Alan fiddled with the controls and wondered aloud if the grate could be got working again. The Agent's young lady sighed and stood tapping her feet. She had summed us up with a glance. She wasn't interested in people who would actually consider *living* in this little hovel. This was a prime site, with great potential for someone with the money to push the little place down and build a proper house. She went and sat in her car whilst we wandered around the garden. We found the old chap's stone-built toolshed and vegetable garden—overgrown with chickweed and groundsel. His blackcurrant bushes were producing well but his roses needed cutting back. We wondered about the apple trees—gnarled, bent and lichen covered. Were they perhaps an old Somerset variety?

We didn't go to the auction but we heard later that the cottage and acre of garden had fetched a price that delighted the Auctioneers and the old man's family.

After about a year of looking we decided that prospective sellers of houses could be classified into three distinct groups, according to age. The young couple (let me call them Julie and Jonathan) were usually selling their house either because it was now too small for their growing family or because Jonathan's work required him to move. The most refreshing thing about Julie and Jonathan was their apparent honesty. I can't make up my mind whether this was because:

    (a) they were inexperienced at selling property,

    (b) they were so confident of their ability to sell they didn't give a damn what you thought of the place, or

    (c) the young are naturally honest,

but we always found that Julie agreed to any viewing time to suit us and obviously made no special effort to clear up. Kicking aside the plastic toys she would cheerfully offer us a cup of coffee, then show us into cluttered bedrooms with unmade beds, and open cupboard doors without embarrassment at the torrent of junk that fell out. Generally speaking Julie and Jonathan didn't do much repair work on their cottage, but they fitted it out with carriage lamps, bogus bottle-glass windows and reproduction stable half-doors. And their choice of decoration was either wallpaper of William Morrissy leaves and flowers, or emulsion paint in shades of purple or orange.

We once looked over a 300-year old cottage in Gloucestershire. It was overlooking a common and surrounded by woodland yet Julie and Jonathan wished to move out because they were homesick for their old town life. They had done all the right things. There was a goat and some contented looking chickens in the orchard, the vegetable garden was productive and well cared for and the whole family had bicycles which they used for cycling around the lanes. There was a wood-burning stove in the lounge, together with Julie's spinning wheel on which she spun wool the family had gathered locally from the hedges and fences. There was a homely smell of cooked flapjacks in the kitchen and Julie, in her peasant skirt and apron, was busy making bread when we arrived. The whole family looked cosily warm in their hand-knitted pullovers, but they all seemed to be sad and bored. They were missing the streets, shops and cultural excitements of Swindon.

We didn't buy their cottage. It was right at the top of our price limit and it had too many snags—some of which were pointed out by Jonathan. It wasn't so much that the Rayburn had been faultily installed and didn't work—(Julie had cooked her flapjacks in the Calor gas cooker)—or that there was a rather worm-eaten roof timber that Jonathan said 'should be looked at'. (We know that 300-year old oak timbers can stand quite a bit of worm chewing.) It was the problem with the chimney. Jonathan explained that because of the way the wood-burning stove had been installed it was impossible to clean the chimney from the bottom and he always climbed upon the roof and pushed the brush down the chimney. In his time Alan has done quite a bit of scrambling about on roofs—repairing stacks, replacing chimney pots and the like—but having now reached his three score years and ten he wasn't keen on the idea of this particular method of chimney sweeping. We left Julie and Jonathan with their problems, their idyllic lifestyle and their sadness.

When we visited houses being sold by people I shall call Ron and Doreen we were greeted in a totally different manner. Smooth and self-assured, Ron was able to point out all the benefits of living in his house and he usually had the previous year's fuel bills and council charges all ready to show us. But we were always wary and ill at ease. Ron and Doreen were probably very nice people but we always had difficulty in believing their reasons for wishing to move. In late middle age, maybe coming up to retirement, the reasons given were usually 'the garden's a bit too much for Ron because of his back trouble', or 'the steps are difficult for Doreen's arthritis', or 'we want to live nearer the children', but we were never convinced. Ron did all the talking. Doreen usually simpered in the background. If she did start to speak Ron looked nervous. 'The council are very good here about keeping the road drains clear' Doreen said once. Being wide-eyed, twittery and with a blue-rinse perm, one would have thought that road drains didn't feature much in Doreen's range of interests. But the cottage was below road level on a bend at the bottom of a steep hill. Doreen had said enough.

If Ron assured us that they used to have marvellous fires in the lounge, 'but we don't bother much since we've had the central heating' we could be fairly sure that there was trouble with the flue. If a cowl was fitted to the chimney pot we knew they had down-draughts. When we once looked over a charming cottage with a grape vine growing up the wall and Doreen coyly pointed out the demijohn sitting prominently on the kitchen table, we assumed, naturally, that it was filled with pink coloured water. We just didn't believe anything they said.

Now when elderly people wish to move the reason is usually obvious. If Herbert and Cynthia have lived in their cottage all their married life then it has to be something drastic and unpleasant that forces them to put it up for sale. A proposed bypass cutting through the garden? A council tip opening up nearby? Nasty neighbours who send highly-amplified thumping electronic noises through the wall? Sometimes Herbert and Cynthia made gently unconvincing attempts at deception, but their worried harassed faces gave them away. We were sorry for them and almost felt guilty that we weren't going to buy their cottage. But more often than not Herbert and Cynthia were no longer together when the house was put on the market. One of them had died and the other wished to move to sheltered accommodation of some sort.

We once looked over a bungalow where Herbert lived alone. He had been a widower for ten years and, now in his 80s, he was cheerfully coming to terms with the fact that his body was failing and his memory was unreliable. When he showed us around his overgrown garden he frequently stumbled over hidden stones or roots, and when he took us indoors I noticed the little memory joggers written in red ink around the place. 'Mr & Mrs West at 11.00 am' said the one on the hall table. 'Immersion heater on' warned the large card on the floor of the passage. 'Casserole in oven' was propped up on the draining board in the kitchen. Herbert was a very interesting person to talk to and he spent more time showing us his collection of antique clocks than showing us around his bungalow. The fact was, he didn't really want to sell it. But his daughter who lived the other side of the country had ear-marked an old person's flat for him; she wanted him to live nearby so that she could keep an eye on him. 'What if you fell down and there's no-one there to pick you up?' was her concern. Herbert wasn't at all bothered at the thought that he might one day be found dead on the carpet (or, more likely, in the garden). He couldn't see that it mattered much. He hoped we wouldn't buy his bungalow. We didn't. And we hope no-one else did either.

As the months went by we began to realise that any house which could be described as a 'cottage' was probably unaffordable or unappealing. Any cottage that we *could* afford was likely to be much too small, hemmed in by others or in such a state of disrepair that we couldn't contemplate living there. Prices of 'cottages' were unbelievable. A small damp terraced 19th-century miners' cottage in a village would be priced at about £10,000 more than the small damp terraced house newly-built on the housing estate nearby. So this was why, having returned from the Forest of Dean after disappointing visits to 'Cosy Cot' and 'The Laurels' we looked again at that Agent's leaflet describing the dull-looking brick built house we had kept passing. The house was big enough for us and there was, apparently, about half an acre of garden. We decided to go and have a look.

It was another golden October afternoon. Oak leaves were pattering down as we got out of the car and we scrunched our way through them to the front door. A robin was singing from the roof. Apart from these gentle sounds there was silence all around us. We were shown first of all into the sitting room where there was a log fire burning in the grate; the flames dancing up the chimney. This was a good start. There was obviously nothing wrong with the flue. I wandered to the end of the room where a glass door overlooked the rear garden and I stopped in astonishment. I don't know whether my mouth fell open but it might have. The garden sloped away from the house—*mainly laid to lawn*—and at the bottom I could see some trees and a tangled hedge. But in the centre of the plot, about two-thirds of the way down, stood one of the most magnificent oak trees I have ever seen. It had a massive trunk with great limbs arching out, almost symetrically, either side. The tree canopy was huge—high, perfectly rounded and in the Autumn sunshine it was a glittering, twinkling spectacle of green and gold. I don't know how long I stood there gaping but I didn't take in much of the rest of the house. I gained the impression that the rooms were light and airy and that the place was big enough for us. But every time I passed a window at the back of the house I had to look again at that tree. And to think, that by just signing a few papers, we could become its guardians. We couldn't possibly *own* the tree but, for a few years hopefully, it could own us. It must have been standing there for a few hundred years and it could march on through time for several more hundred years. Perhaps we could be privileged to see it through the last years of the 20th century and into the 21st century.

Alan, of course, saw other things. Outside the house he saw that the woodwork, plastic guttering, downpipes, fascias and soffits had been covered with white emulsion paint. Inside the house he noticed cracked plaster, wrinkled wallpaper and doors which he later described to me as 'hardboard-faced hollow crap'. But he too warmed his hands at the log fire, and he too looked in awe at The Oak.

It didn't take much discussion. We had found our patch.

CHAPTER 2

The Homestead

I can't think of anything complimentary to say about this house, so perhaps the less said the better. It was built in the early 1960s, under government contract, to accommodate a Forestry Commission worker and his family. We get the strong impression that the chaps engaged on the building work hated their job and didn't think much of each other either. Everywhere we look we find evidence of bad temper, and workmanship of such incompetence that we almost begin to suspect malicious intent. Take, for example, the chap responsible for the rainwater fittings. He obviously wasn't on speaking terms with the roofer and he fastened the guttering to the fascias before the tiles were in place, with the result that a lot of the rainwater which poured down the roof managed to miss the guttering and spewed out over the path. In view of the lack of space between tile edges and guttering it was impossible to get at any of the fixing screws, or to insert a hand to remove any leaves and other debris, which didn't make any difference anyway because the gutter-installer, by skilfully arranging the gutter to slope the wrong way, managed to ensure that during a heavy rainstorm any rain that in fact managed to get into his gutter only found its way to the down-pipe when the guttering had become full to the brim and was over-flowing at the other end (or, in one place, onto the back door step). We think he must have been in league with the bloke who laid all the paving slabs around the house. They all slope very slightly towards the house, thus ensuring that the water pouring off the roof collects in long lakes against the house walls.

There is one good thing to say about the house. It is built, mainly, of excellent quality bricks. They are extremely hard—as Alan found when he tried to drill into them. Unfortunately the chap laying them either had an unsteady hand or didn't believe in wearing his glasses on the job. The courses of bricks wave in and out. He managed to get a reasonably straight horizontal line and his wavering workmanship is not noticeable when looking at the wall face on. But it's best not to stand alongside the walls gazing upwards in slanting sunshine, moonlight or after dark when the outside light is on. The walls gently undulate in and out from path level up to soffits.

The inside workmen didn't seem to be a happy bunch either. The chap fixing the window stays so arranged them that only two holes could be used—the window has either to be wide open or shut—and the painter couldn't wait for the joiner to finish before he started slapping on the paint. How else can one account for the splinters, gobbets of sawdust and general muck that is stuck firmly by gloss paint to all skirting boards and door frames? And on the subject of door frames, many of them are so constructed to encourage a collision with the base of the door below the bottom hinge. Hardboard-faced hollow doors subject to such squeezing usually break at the bottom. We haven't yet worked out what to do about this, although we have got around some of the door problems by simply removing them. There were twenty-four doors in the house when we arrived—all poorly constructed, some unnecessary and some so arranged that they fouled each other when opened. The double doors leading from the porch to the hall were a good example of doors designed to encourage maximum irritation. The porch appears to have been an after-thought—it is so poorly constructed that we think the contractor was running short of money at this stage—and you pushed through a pair of narrow glass doors to get into the house. The doors may have been narrow, but so too is the hallway and having pushed through them there was nowhere to go except up the stairs. You could turn neither left nor right until one of the doors was closed.

Somehow, we were going to make a home out of this.

The main house has two rooms downstairs, of reasonable size and pleasant proportions, and three bedrooms and a bathroom upstairs. But there is a single-storey annexe to the house which contains a 12ft. x 10ft. room leading on to a passageway, a lavatory, a 6ft. x 8ft.

room (which we are told was the Forester's office and is now Alan's workshop) and the garage. The 12ft. x 10ft. room leads directly into the back garden and we immediately decided that this would be an ideal room in which to hang old clothes, take off wellington boots, store pumpkins, marrows and shallots etc., dump baskets and bowls, keep the preserving pan, washing machine, spin dryer, clothes basket, Primus stoves, paraffin and methylated spirits, fix up the ceiling clothes rack and accommodate a long bench seat under which the walking boots could be lined up. Unfortunately a previous occupant of the house had decided that this room was to be her kitchen and it was filled with fitted units. In the pale indeterminate colours that these units often come in—'Blue Fantasy'?, 'Whisper Grey'?, 'Dawn Haze'?—they lined all sides of the room and stuck out from the walls. They looked quite new but they were in the way and they had to go. Alan salvaged some of the chipboard worktops which he thought he might find a use for, and he also removed all the (very high quality) china knobs. But the cupboards, drawers and wobbly sidepieces were pulled out and disposed of. With the units removed we were able to see the tangled mess of wires and plumbing (some of it obviously dating back to the 1960s) the holes in the walls and the crumbling concrete floor—mouldy and damp from years of water seeping from kitchen lino underneath fitted units. Having pulled out the sink unit Alan decided to clean and re-instal the sink as it would be a useful place for cleaning paint brushes and washing out flower pots. So we worked the first winter chipping off pink wall tiles, renewing wiring and plumbing, filling in holes, repairing concrete and finally painting the walls and sticking down an all-over vinyl floor covering which allowed of no cracks between the repaired skirting boards and the floor. I say 'we' worked, but in fact it was Alan who did it all. I was merely his assistant. All down the years I have been his assistant. My instructions are the same now as they have always been—'Pass me that tool'; 'Hang onto the other end of this plank'; 'Stand on the bottom of this ladder'; 'Hold this while I hit it'—but now my first job is to go and find his glasses. And the coffee breaks, these days, seem to be more frequent and last longer. Nevertheless, we ended up with a bright, attractive and useful room which we've now filled with old clothes, wellington boots, stored vegetables, etc. etc. We refer to it as the 'back kitchen'.

The room leading from the main house into the back kitchen had obviously, at one time, been divided in two, with a 'kitchen end' with sink and walk-in cupboard, and a 'dining room' end with a fireplace. The division between the two rooms had been removed (which we thought was a good idea), but the sink had also been removed and the fireplace filled in (which we didn't think was a good idea). The window at the 'kitchen end' with its view down the garden, was surely the obvious place to have a sink, and the chimney breast was the obvious place to instal a heat retention cooker. This room was to be our kitchen, and, in our view, the kitchen is the most important room in the house.

In the early days of our marriage I used to day-dream about the ideal kitchen that I planned to have one day. I knew exactly what I wanted. It was depicted, more or less, in a drawing in the front of my cookery book showing a farmhouse kitchen, complete with ceiling beams, lattice windows and a large black range. There is a cheerful fire burning in the range; a cooking pot sits nearby, ornaments clutter a high mantleshelf and comfortable chairs surround the hearth. I could imagine nothing more homely and appealing than sitting alongside that fire, my feet upon the fender, a bowl of peas in my lap to shell and a kettle singing upon the hearth. This ideal kitchen came within my grasp when, after five years of living in a town flat, we bought that primitive cottage in North Wales. There was, to my delight, a range in the kitchen. But it wasn't an old black range, it was a newish (probably 1950s) cream and green cast-iron 'combination grate' with two ovens and an open fire. It was called (according to the dignified cast-iron label on the front) The Chatham Special.

Unfortunately, whoever had installed it hadn't done the job properly. No matter how large a fire we had roaring up the chimney the ovens got only to plate-warming temperature. Moreover, roaring evening fires turned into cold grey ashes by morning and, in a house with no electricity, someone had to get up and light the fire before we could have a cup of tea. That cold damp cottage needed a permanent source of warmth and it wasn't getting it from The Chatham Special. So we then started thinking about heat retention cookers, and we found exactly what we wanted—the Esse Wellstood stove. It had a long hotplate, two ovens (one hot and one slow) and a 16-

14

gallon side hot water tank. We topped this up each day with a few buckets filled at the spring and had a non-stop supply of near-boiling water. The stove was fuelled by coal, wood, peat or any old rubbish, and the side-tank provided ample plate-warming space. The kettle, kept to one side, instantly boiled when slid along the hotplate in the morning, and when the wind was in the right direction we could leave the fire door open and enjoy the sight of the flaming coals. For thirteen years it was the soul of the cottage and the centre of our life. When our circumstances changed and we had to return to live in town I left our moorland home with tears of regret. Some of those tears were shed for my Esse Wellstood stove that had to stay behind.

For the next fifteen years we lived in suburbia and I cooked on a gas stove (in a fitted kitchen, like everyone else) but as soon as we bought *this* house we started on a tour of showrooms to look for another heat retention cooker. We discovered that they were now available fuelled by gas, electricity and oil as well as solid fuel. There was a choice between a large variety of designs and colours, all with the old-fashioned 'cottagey' appearance, but we found none made to the old fashioned standards. Cookers claiming to be made of cast iron seemed to have quite a bit of sheet steel in them. We noticed oven handles made of plastic. Nuts, bolts and screws protruded from some stoves and some had ill-fitting doors where the edges had not been properly ground off. One cooker had an alarming hotplate cover that would barely stay upright when raised. Moreover, the new designs seemed to be very complicated with a confusion of knobs, lights and dials and with thermostats that clicked and thumped into action and burners that roared.

We didn't like anything that we saw. We wanted another stove like the Wellstood that just sat in the kitchen quietly getting on with its job and making no noises except for the occasional shifting of coal in the firebox and the sound of the wind in the chimney. We knew that the Wellstood was no longer available, but we had decided anyway that with old age ahead of us we didn't want the chore of looking after a solid fuel appliance. Nor (in an area prone to power cuts) did we want to be dependent upon electricity. Was it not possible to buy a silent uncomplicated oil-burning cooker? It was.

We discovered an enterprising establishment that ran a successful business restoring original Aga and Rayburn cookers and converting them to suit their customers' requirements. These old cookers were so well made they could stand up to all the rough treatment necessary to bash them out of houses where they weren't wanted and refurbish them for installing in houses where they were. Prospective customers could save about £1,000 (on the price of a similar but new cooker) and could have the satisfaction of knowing that they are part of a very worthwhile recycling operation. We chose a two-oven Aga in traditional cream colour with a gravity-fed wick burner, and we now have homely comfort in our kitchen once again.

Of course I made immediate uncharitable comparisons with our old Esse Wellstood. We think that one long hotplate with graduated heat and one oblong lid is more efficient and easier to use than two round hot-plates, and there was more plate-warming room on top of the Wellstood. The Aga oven rails are awkward to use as they catch and judder on the lugs at the side, and I'm not too sure about this special flue arrangement in the ovens whereby no cooking smells permeate the kitchen. Certainly it is an advantage not to have the place reeking of kippers or soused mackerel but we miss the smells of baking bread and savoury stuffings. What's more, a burning cake can go unnoticed and forgotten. But I must admit that a vented bottom oven is an advantage. A casserole in my Wellstood would soon send a trickle of condensation down the outside of the cooker, to collect in a puddle on the floor. No such trickle comes from the Aga.

We turn off the Aga once a year for servicing and renewal of the wicks. A telephone call brings the oil delivery to our tank in the garden and, day and night, and independent of electricity, we have the comforting presence of a heat retention cooker in the kitchen. We dry herbs over it, hang laundry in front of it and warm hats and gloves on top of it. We sit alongside it, lean against it and kneel in front of it. And, apart from the sound of the wind in the chimney, it is silent. It's not the Esse Wellstood—but it will do.

This determination to live in comfort without being dependent upon electricity stems from the early years of our marriage when we were not connected to any mains supplies but were never cold, hungry or without light. But this attitude has meant that we have both been rather slow in equipping ourselves with electricial appliances. I was 40 years old before I bought a vacuum cleaner and we only went in for a refrigerator when we moved into a centrally heated house that had no larder. (We still have that refrigerator. It lives in the back kitchen but is only in use during warm weather. When the temperature in the back kitchen drops to 42°F there is no point in running a refrigerator.) I was in my 60s before it occurred to me to buy a washing machine, and Alan was nearly 70 when he (with great reluctance) equipped himself with a few power tools. I was very glad when he decided to buy a couple of electrically-powered grinders. Previously his grinder had been wife-powered and I must admit to begrudging the time spent turning the handle whilst he put an edge upon shears, plane irons, scissors, chisels and drills. We have no electrical gadgets in the kitchen, and we have not yet felt the need of a deep freeze cabinet, a micro-wave oven, a dish-washer or a television set.

I am very fond of my four cast-iron flat irons. Two of them have the word 'Canon' incorporated within the casting so presumably they date from the early gas stove era. I keep these as spares because I prefer the other two. One bears the words 'J & S Siddons, West Bromwich' but the other one has nothing upon it but the number 5. This one is my favourite. It would appear to be much older than the others. It is as smooth as glass, fits snugly into my hand and glides beautifully over all my laundry. Once, on a cold dank November afternoon when I was doing the ironing we had a power cut but I didn't realise it until I decided that it was getting rather dim in the kitchen and I went to switch on the light. Nothing happened. So I went and looked out of the kitchen window. When the leaves start falling from the trees we can see the roofs and lights of the village in the valley below, but all was in darkness down there. Obviously the Midlands Electricity Board had cut off the supply once again. So I lit the Aladdin lamp we have fixed to the wall alongside the Aga and I carried on ironing, smug in the knowledge that the casserole and jacket potatoes in the oven would carry on cooking. We have an elegant Aladdin table lamp that I planned to light for the dinner table, and I was almost disappointed when the power was restored about twenty minutes later.

But although I can sneer at the Midlands Electricity Board's service in the winter I know that life would be rather difficult without it in summer. During the very hot months when the sun beats without mercy into this valley we turn off the Aga. Thereafter, until the cooler days of Autumn, I cook in the back kitchen upon a very small (table model) electric stove and I do my ironing with an electric iron trailing a lead—the same as everyone else. Although most of our summer frying and boiling is done in the back kitchen upon our trusty twin-burner Primus stove I know I could not manage without an electric oven. I haven't yet figured out a way of baking bread on a Primus.

We have a variety of paraffin lamps and stoves that have been with us all our married life and, like all possessions that give good service, we have a special affection for them. When I stop comparing the Aga with the Esse Wellstood I shall no doubt become very fond of it, and I sometimes wonder about the person who owned it before us. What sort of kitchen did the Aga warm before it came here? Did the previous owner sit, like me, alongside the stove with a forearm resting upon a warm surface and did she, like me, discover that to squat in front of the cooker with your lower back against the bottom oven door is a most soothing thing to do for an aching back? I say 'she' because I think that these old Agas must have been designed for female cooks. The handles to the hotplate covers are so narrow that any man with a large hand might find them awkward to use. But, when thinking about all the various bits of second-hand equipment we use I wonder mostly about the women who, down the ages, have used my favourite flat iron. It is probably well over a hundred years old and it has obviously smoothed a lot of laundry in its time. As I wander between Aga and ironing table, my knitted kettle holder in hand, changing over my irons as they cool, I feel a sisterly affection for those long-dead homely women who once used my flat irons.

But that's enough whimsey. There's nothing whimsical about plumbing, and that was our first real problem here.

The system was very complicated. There were numerous water tanks in the roof (I now forget how many) including, for some strange reason, a hot water cylinder in the roof void above the garage. This meant that water from this cylinder had to cross the house cavity wall and this pipe froze up within three months of us moving in. There was an oil-fired central heating system which ran fourteen radiators one of which, curiously, was in the cupboard under the stairs. There was a network of water pipes in roof voids and under the bathroom and bedroom floorboards. Not all of these pipes contained water and we were unable to work out which fed what going where. We decided to have the lot ripped out and start again.

Having at one time been happy enough to carry all water in buckets from a spring to the kitchen I am sufficiently grateful in old age to have mains water brought into the house for me not to quibble too much about its quality. (I don't know about your supply, but we wouldn't dream of drinking ours without boiling it.)

Finding a large double-drainer sink for the kitchen was another difficulty. All the new sinks we looked at were just about big enough for washing hankies or swilling out a tea cup and I knew that there was no way in which I could wash my preserving pan in such a sink. So we started looking for a second-hand sink and even cast thoughtful eyes at the crumbling and damaged Belfast sink that was out in the garden and which, I suppose, a previous occupant of the house had removed from the kitchen. But, having got other members of the family searching their local paper advertisements, my sister found us a perfectly satisfactory stainless steel double-drainer sink in excellent condition, for which she paid £5. (And I suppose the woman who had this removed from her kitchen is now managing with an inferior little basin that happened to come with her 'Blue Fantasy', 'Whisper Grey' or 'Dawn Haze' units.)

Our house heating system is as basic and simple as our plumbing. The Aga heats the kitchen and the bedroom above, an open fire heats the sitting room, and in each other room of the main house we have a variety of electric heaters which are switched on when the room is in use. When we use electrical heating we are lavish with it. Sometimes when there is a bitterly cold north-east wind howling around the house we use some back-up electrical heat in the sitting room. But there are only two of us in this house and we see no point in heating rooms that are unoccupied. We realise that our system wouldn't appeal to many people. If you came to visit us in the winter you would probably complain of the draught in the sitting room and you might feel obliged to wear balaclava and overcoat when visiting the bathroom, but the system suits us. We don't reckon on spending very much time in the bathroom each day, and for the time that we *are* there and stripped off, we have an efficient wall-mounted electric fan heater which sends out a most satisfying blast of hot air.

Gradually, with the passing of the years, we are turning this house into a home. Into all odd corners of the rooms Alan has fixed shelves which he has made from oak, rosewood or mahogany (for the sitting room and kitchen) and rubbishy bits of plywood and chipboard (for the bedrooms and back kitchen). And if Alan fixes shelves, I will fill them—mostly with books. It is only when you have worked upon a place that it begins to feel like yours. Most of the windows have now been replaced—sawing up the old wooden frames to burn on the fire gave me great satisfaction—and most of the roof guttering has been renewed and now slopes the correct way. (In order to get at the fixing screws of the old guttering the nails securing the bottom row of tiles had to be ripped out and the tiles moved.)

But there are some things we can't alter and are learning to live with—like the badly cast and out-of-line concrete drain gullies around the house—and we are still coming up against evidence of sloppy workmanship. I was puzzled by the little piles of rock-hard cement that are on the path at various places around the house near the walls, but Alan guessed what they were. He reckons that the chap pointing up the house walls was a disgruntled worker and that as soon as clocking-off time came he knocked out his trowel upon the path, said 'Sod it' and went home. And there, for the thirty odd years since, those little piles of cement have stayed where he left them.

But that's enough about the house. Let's go out into the garden.

CHAPTER 3

A Plot of Land

A pleasant thing about most cottage gardens is their higgledy-piggledy shape. Boundary hedges and walls sometimes take dog-leg turns, often for no apparent reason, and an overgrown hedge can disappear into a very large bramble patch with no-one being quite sure where the boundary is. We once went to see a cottage where the Agent showing us around told us that a bit of land in the adjoining field went with the cottage. 'You own the bit from this hedge across to the hawthorn tree, and then diagonally across to the footpath' he said. There were no other physical markers in the field to identify the cottage's 'bit'. But no-one locally was concerned about this. That 'bit' had always gone with the cottage. There had never been any arguments about the matter. We have looked at cottages where the back garden sprawled across what should have been the neighbour's patch and where the front garden was on the other side of the lane. All very charming—if somewhat inconvenient.

There were no such inconvenient charms here. With this house the Forestry Commission had allocated an almost rectangular strip running from east to west down the slope. Another charming thing about most cottage gardens is that, more often than not, they contain outbuildings—old stone pigsties, corrugated iron roofed chicken houses, fuel stores and bike shelters—all useful places in which to store wire netting, logs, spare slates, bits of timber, wheelbarrow, lawn mower, garden tools and all the stacks of useful junk that no cottager can manage without.

There were no outbuildings here—not even a garden shed, and the large amount of useful junk that we have been carrying around for most of our married life had to be squashed into the garage, Alan's workshop, the downstairs lavatory, the back kitchen and a bedroom. When the tatty white-emulsion-painted guttering and downpipes were removed from the house Alan insisted on keeping it all as it 'might come in useful'. It did—eventually. But for about a year it lay in an unlovely heap on the lawn at the back of the house. We kept on moving it around to less visually intrusive places but it then became in the way of some particularly urgent work and had to be carted back to the lawn.

According to the details we had received from the Agent this rectangular strip was 'almost half an acre' but one day Alan decided that we would measure it, using a surveyor's tape which was rather frayed and elderly, albeit in a handsome leather and brass case. According to the measurements thus taken this plot, according to Alan, is nearer three-eighths of an acre than half. I have to take his word for it. He was the one with the clipboard making the notes; I was the one who took the frayed end of the tape through the nettles and brambles to reach the post-and-wire fence. All I know is that if you are standing at the bottom of the garden with a large bough of fallen oak that you want to drag up the slope to the sawbench then it seems a very long way. I am quite happy to accept the Agent's description of 'nearly half an acre'.

Whilst we were at the bottom of the garden with the tape measure we decided to measure the large oak tree. Scrambling about on its lumpy rooted base we took a measurement around the girth at about the height of 5ft. It measured 12ft. 6ins. which means, according to a Forestry Commission official we consulted, that the tree has been growing here for 250 to 300 years. It has our profound admiration and respect. I feel I should curtsy every time I pass it.

Having in the past cultivated a garden at 1,000ft. above sea level on an exposed moorland in North Wales and also one on a highly polluted plot at almost sea level between the A38 and a chemical works, we felt we were now well qualified to assess the possible benefits and snags of any prospective garden. With our present plot of land in the Forest we reckoned we were going to have to cope with two definite problems but would enjoy one tremendous advantage.

A PLOT OF LAND

Thus:

1. This plot, on its downward slope east to west, surrounded by Forest trees will not get much direct sunlight. (*Right*. On sunny winter mornings we sometimes look with envious eyes to the other side of the valley where we can see the forest in full sunshine—the rusty coloured larches, the dark swathes of conifers and the bare-boughed oaks all softly lit in a golden light, whilst we continue shivering in dank shade. It will be at least another hour before the sun first touches the top of The Oak and then creeps gradually down to the garden.)

2. This plot, on a slope overlooking a valley through which runs a small river will no doubt be subject to frosts and rising mists. (*Right*. Sometimes we look down upon the mist swirling around between the trees in the valley bottom, but often it creeps up the slope to engulf us, and the frosts are the most severe we have ever encountered anywhere before. They come early (sometimes in September) and they come late (sometimes in June). For days on end in winter the ground is rock hard; all foliage is whitened and all water is frozen. Only the hardiest plants can survive.)

3. This plot, on a piece of land that was formerly woodland, will have a deep rich soil full of nutrients from the many layers of leaf mould. (*Wrong*. As the entire plot was *laid to lawn* when we took over we had no way of knowing how cultivatable the ground was. But when Alan first plunged a spade into the turf he lifted up half a brick, some ashes, four old toothpaste tubes and a bit of wire. He tried again, a few yards away, and found himself with some more broken brick, a pile of stones, broken glass and a few plastic clothes pegs. We later learned that in order to build the house on this slope a fleet of lorries had brought load after load of rubbish-tip spoil in order to get a fairly level site. This spoil covers the whole of the top of the garden—which is the only area which gets any significant amount of sunshine.)

The underlying subsoil here is clay—thick, greasy yellow stuff which we found ourselves levering up when we tried to get beneath a thin layer of topsoil mixed with can ring-pulls, crisp packets, old toothbrushes and broken crockery, and it surprised us that even at the bottom of the garden (out of reach of the tipping lorries) we were coming across evidence of man's interference. There are ridges and furrows, and what we first thought were lumps of natural rock turned out to be dressed stone. But we are now surprised that we were surprised because all down the centuries man has been interfering with the Forest of Dean. The hunting of the deer and the felling of the trees has been going on alongside charcoal burning, coal mining, iron ore mining, iron smelting and tin plate making—all of them nasty, dirty, noisy activities leaving behind them piles of slag and cinders. You can't walk far in the Forest without tripping over an old tramline or stumbling into a charcoal pit. But it is all green and silent now. Most scars are covered with a healing blanket of bracken and foxglove. At the bottom of our garden the scars seem to be mostly covered with a healing blanket of dock, nettles, cocksfoot and tussock grass, and when planting some hyacinth bulbs down there one day we discovered the remains of a cinder tip. However, when grovelling about in it with spade and trowel I unearthed from amongst the cinders a Victorian penny dated 1898—a much more interesting discovery than the split detergent bottles, squashed lager cans and bits of old cable to be found further up the slope.

The first thing one does when taking over a new garden is to find out what is already growing there. In the front garden here there were a couple of cotoneaster bushes, a quince, a large white-flowered veronica shrub and a viburnum *laurustinus*. At first I didn't particularly like the *laurustinus*; it is too Municipal Parkish. But I have changed my mind. Being evergreen and with a good high rounded canopy, it provides excellent shelter for the birds and its white rosettes of flowers look cheerful in the winter. Moreover, at the end of February I have seen a few early foraging wild bees finding food there. The veronica bush is high and unruly and, because it overhangs the front gate, it has constantly to be cut back. But I forgive it everything because it is covered in long clusters of flowers from late spring until late Autumn and the butterflies love it.

On either side of the garden at the back were two long lines of closely planted Western red cedar trees which were obviously meant to be a hedge but had been neglected and were now probably 30ft. high and waved around furiously in the wind. These lines of trees stopped short about halfway down the garden—the one side ending in a forsythia bush and the other side at a sumac tree.

Beyond that the wire and post fence carried on to the bottom of the garden. Near the back door there was a mallow bush (which died in the first frost) and a dwarf rhododendron. The post and wire fences were erratically tangled up with brambles and at one place there was a small stand of raspberries which I thought were the delightfully tasting wild ones but turned out to be cultivated ones gone wild which isn't the same thing at all. But the whole area at the end of the garden is dominated by four oak trees. The Oak stands centrally in the plot and it is only when you pass beneath its huge arching boughs you become aware of the other three oak trees standing somewhat apologetically at the bottom of the garden. In his book *The History of the Countryside* Oliver Rackham relates that in the 19th century the Dean foresters of the time thought they were doing the right thing by getting rid of all the indigenous oak trees and replacing them with allegedly superior *quercus robur* from elsewhere. They were wrong. The introduced trees have not prospered and (according to a local Forester we have talked with) the trees easily become diseased and have been of no use for timber. Well, those three trees at the bottom of our garden are not prospering and it would appear that they are some of those rubbishy *quercus robur*. It looks as though some ham-fisted pollarding has been attempted at one time, quite a few rotten branches have fallen off in the past and there are obviously a few more of them up there to come down. These are typical of the oak trees you can now see all around the Forest of Dean. There are very few of the original mighty oaks of old England. You will find some in the Speech House area, and we think you'll find another one halfway down our garden.

There are two apple trees in the garden. Neither of the trees is very old but one is growing sturdily and in our first year here it produced three well-shaped large green apples. The other one, which was planted irritatingly in the centre of the garden not more than 19 yards up the slope from The Oak, stood about 3ft. high and consisted of a poker-thick trunk and three spindly twigs which couldn't possibly be called branches. It was irritating because it was right in your line of vision when looking down the garden towards The Oak. Just like having something stuck in the corner of your eye. Being too busy with other things we didn't get around to doing anything about this tree for a few years, during which time it produced a yearly crop of about five tiny bright red apples, all of which appeared to have some disease and all of which dropped off before the end of the summer. As we were unable to identify these trees (we still haven't) we usually referred to the larger one as the cooker and the other as the eater. Alan pruned 'the cooker' and gave it a good dressing of manure. He occasionally feeds it with wood ash and it has since then provided us with a good harvest of large green apples that remain firm when cooked, are tasty, and keep well during the winter.

He finally got around to doing something about 'the eater' last Autumn. He dug it up, took it to the side of the garden (where it would get slightly more sun) and planted it near the fence. He gave it some bonemeal, a good dressing of manure, staked its spindly trunk and told it to get on with it—live or die. The spring following this injunction the little tree broke into blossom all along each twiggy branch. We counted 44 blooms. Once the bees had finished their work we removed all but three little apples—allowing the tree to keep one per branch. Those three little green apples grew and grew and became so large that I felt obliged to pick them at the beginning of October as the fruit was obviously becoming too heavy for the branches to support. As we had always called this tree 'the eater' we tried nibbling one. It was exceedingly sharp and sour so we decided that our eater was in fact another cooker, and I put the remaining two apples in store with those from the other tree. One of these apples has remained green and hard; the other is turning a mellow yellow with faint red stripes. Is this perhaps what is known as a 'family tree' (which produces eaters and cookers on the same stock)? We shall have to wait and see.

The only other tree in the garden was a graceful common birch, growing near the south boundary about 30 yards from the sitting room windows, but none of the trees and shrubs already here disguised the fact that this was a rectangular plot on a slope. We were going to have to do something about this.

We had three main desires. We wanted flowers, shrubs and plants that were scented, beautiful and interesting. We wanted vegetables and we wanted an area of ground to be left to its own devices so that we could watch what would happen. Oak tree grove was obviously the patch of ground to leave alone. We do very little down there except occasionally cut some of the grass, and the whole area is known to us as 'the rough' and it finishes just behind The Oak. The area of grass between The Oak and the main apple tree is mown three or four times a year and we call it 'the meadow'. The idea here is that small creeping plants will be encouraged to flourish, and the appearance of a gradually expanding patch of violets has proved that this was a very good idea. To mark the boundary of the meadow and the rough we have planted a curving line of dogwood, buddleia and veronica cuttings, all of which have settled down and are sprouting vigorously. We grow vegetables in the patch of ground overlooked by the kitchen window, and we grow flowers, shrubs and interesting plants everywhere.

First of all we had to do something about those neglected cedar hedges. Alan decided that an acceptable height for a cedar hedge would be about 7ft. so he got out his saw and stepladder to tackle the job the first February after we had moved in. But some of those cedar trunks now had a diameter of about 7ins.; some were dead, some were ragged where bits had been cut off in the past, and all were surrounded in twangy bits of leafy twig that perpetually caught in the saw blade. It was not an easy job and it took several weeks. His method of working was to lean the ladder against a chosen cedar trunk then cut it (and any nearby ones he could reach) at the desired height, having first of all tied a rope to the tree being cut a few feet above the level of his saw. My job was to hang onto the other end of the rope and, when told that the trunk was nearly severed, to yank it so that it fell to Alan's side and not on top of him. This operation worked successfully until the very last bit was being cut alongside the sumac tree where the cedar was rather large, particularly leafy and my yank a bit premature. The tree, the stepladder, Alan and his saw and the rope came down in a remarkably slow-motion collapse amongst the branches of the sumac, a bramble and the little rhododendron bush we had only recently transplanted there from its original place outside the back door. I could tell, by the impolite words that came from beneath the cedar branches, that no damage had been done to Alan but the little rhododendron bush hasn't been the same since—which only goes to show that we were daft to transplant it there before the hedge had been cut.

Moving the piles of cedar from the lawn was my job—'clearing up after' is usually women's work in this household—and I dragged it all down into the rough where it remained in a large stack to await my further attention. During the following summer and autumn, when I had nothing better to do, I tackled that pile of cedar with secateurs, hatchet and saw and sorted it into a heap of trimmings for the bonfire and a neat stack of poles which I leaned against The Oak. These spent the next year drying out and were eventually sawn into logs for the sitting room fire. Cedar foliage has a pungent fruity scent and, whether green or long-dead-and-gone-brown, it burns with a furious crackling gusto which delights enthusiastic bonfire burners like me. It also makes marvellous kindling. The cedar hedge looked very shorn and barren for a year. One line of trunks was so devoid of any foliage that we called it 'the palisade'. But now those trunks are sprouting little tufts of feathery green foliage, and twigs of greenery are thrusting above the somewhat nominal 7ft. height of the hedge. The palisade is becoming a hedge again.

Once the cedar hedge had been dealt with we started planning and planting. Beyond the sumac and unfortunate rhododendron we planted an *euonymus* (because of its yellow and green leaves), a Korean fir (because we like its purple cones) and a *cryptomeria* (because it looked nice and feathery in the garden centre and the sales lady was persuasive.) We added hazel bushes (transplanted from the vegetable garden and where they keep appearing), a Japanese knotweed (which *we* like, in spite of what the experts say) and a host of other shrubby, showy but scentless things that were in the way elsewhere and this was just the place to bung them. This area is now known as 'the shrubbery' and is beginning to conceal the wire and post fence beyond.

The view from the sitting room is down the slope of the lawn to The Oak, and this lawn is now separated from the vegetable garden by a small hedge of mixed herb bushes. This hedge makes a couple of bold curves before winding down the slope to end near the main apple tree. This apple tree has now been joined by a stand of rhubarb, some gooseberries and a few blackcurrant bushes. We refer to this plot as 'the orchard', beyond which we have planted a curved line of buddleia. And behind this again we have a small patch of land which is now out of sight of the house and upon which I have my bonfire, alongside a stack of wire netting, a collection of rotting-but-still-useful planks and the aforementioned lengths of dirty white guttering and downpipes. The garden was taking shape.

We spent money. We bought pyracantha, dogwood, various artemisias, sages, rosemaries, hyssops and thymes. We made flower borders in any bit of ground that could receive the sun and we planted roses, Michaelmas daisies, red hot pokers, scented peonies, lavenders, pansies, jonquils and other scented narcissi. We made mistakes—like the glowing yellow chrysanthemum which we thought would look nice against the dark greenery of the cedar hedge. It did—for just one season, then we never saw it again; and there was the exquisitely perfumed daphne *mezereum* that slowly withered over two years and then gave up the ghost. We collected the seeds of marigolds, sweet peas, honesty, snapdragons and poppies from other people's gardens, and the seeds of foxgloves from wild places. We had disappointments—like the new-fangled pinks the seed of which was expensive to buy, reluctant to germinate and finally produced some feeble straggling blooms that smelt faintly of cheap talcum powder. The chrysanthemums were a disappointment too. We wanted the hardy old fashioned bronze colour blooms with that special autumnal chrysanthemum scent. We bought seed and we sent away for plants but in every case the blooms were the wrong colour and type and devoid of scent.

Where have all the perfumed flowers gone? Stroll around any florist's shop and have a sniff at the carnations and roses. Nothing. They might as well be made of plastic. When buying our rose bushes we noticed that amongst a wide range of types and colours on offer very few bore labels that suggested the flowers would be scented. But, fortunately, gardeners will make friends with other gardeners and we are finding many friends in the Forest of Dean. Once, in June, I visited one of them and when walking around the side of her bungalow to the back I was brought to an astonished stop by the sight and exquisite perfume of the wide drifts of old-fasioned English pinks growing all around her terrace. I expressed my delight and then had difficulty in stopping my friend from there and then tearing up some plants to give to me. But she didn't forget. Later, in the autumn, we found outside our door a large bag filled with the roots of pinks. We planted them out and they flourished.

We have since divided them and are gradually spreading them around the garden. And every time I am on my knees cutting the lawn edges near a clump of pinks I breathe in that heavenly scent and think of my friend.

It was another friend who gave us the gooseberries. We trundled them back from his garden in a wheelbarrow—huge straggling things that looked too old to move but which have settled down and they give us a good crop of thumping great green gooseberries each year. Another friend gave us the clump of rhubarb and the cuttings from which we have grown our blackcurrants, and it was his wife who gave me the lupins. Seeing the feeble things I was trying to grow from commercial seed she presented me with several potted-up little plants that have now taken over a corner of the front garden. My brother gave us a carrier bag full of hyacinth bulbs and my sister has given us willow cuttings, a hawthorn, honeysuckle and countless other plants most of which have survived and flourished. All around the garden there are plants that remind us of people who have been kind.

But things began to arrive without any help from anyone. An evening primrose appeared one year in the front garden and it has decided to colonise one corner. When pushing the hand mower over the grass once I noticed what appeared to be a patch of cowslips in the turf. It *was* a patch of cowslips. I later discovered yellow pimpernel and pale flax growing there. As soon as we cleared ground for the vegetable garden it seemed that seedlings of sycamore, buddleia, hazel and hawthorn decided that here was a good place to grow. We decided otherwise and moved them else-where. Down in the rough things were happening too. We found that it wasn't *all* docks, nettles, cocksfoot and tussock grass. We found we had vetch, lady's smock, pignuts and a few wild bluebells and violets, all of which increased as the years went by. Hazel, hawthorn, oak and wild cherry saplings appeared—some of which had to be moved to the sides of the garden where they would enjoy more sunshine. It was becoming obvious that, left to its own devices, this plot would become a wild wood again.

It is now not quite so obvious that we have a rectangular piece of land, but the garden has not taken shape entirely by design; some of it has been accidental—like what happened in an area of ground at the base of one of the oak trees at the bottom of the garden. Alan was down there planting daffodils. We had found daffodils coming up in isolated little bunches down in the rough and we decided they would look much better if moved and planted all together down on the cinder tip near the bluebells; the idea being that underneath the oak a drift of daffodils blooming in the spring would be followed by a riot of bluebells. I was dawdling over the washing up and looking out of the window at the same time and it became obvious to me that Alan was having difficulties down there. After a while he abandoned his spade and came up to get his mattock, pickaxe and two crowbars—which seemed a rather desperate way to go about planting a few daffodil bulbs. The washing up got slower and slower as I watched what was going on and it soon became clear that he was getting out stones—huge stones; some of them as big as a hundred-weight sack of coal and probably twice as heavy. (He has since esti-mated that one of these stones must weigh about $3^{1}/_{2}$ cwt.) He raised them up to the surface by means of crowbar, ingenuity and brute force. But, having got them up, he could do no more than roll them to one side, leave them, and get on with the job of planting bulbs. Now this was looking interesting. *Very* interesting. He was unconsciously forming a stone circle down there. One of the stones was tombstone shaped; another pointed a stony finger skywards; another was a dumpy lump (just asking to be sat upon) and he was working in the middle of them. The smaller stones he was taking to the back of his circle and piling them up—cairn like. I could hardly wait for him to return to the house to point out to him the effect of what he had been doing. It reminded me very much of those ancient remains of little stone settlements that can be found on the wilder uplands of Dartmoor. So we have referred to it ever since as the 'hut circle'.

The stones have remained there. They lie in the positions they took up when Alan heaved them out of the earth, and in springtime and summer the daffodils and bluebells bloom prettily between them. But in the winter time they stand alone down there under-neath the bottom oak tree. And I find myself looking at them, and wondering. I know perfectly well that these are lumps of dressed stone that at one time were buried in a cinder pile and that Alan heaved out of the ground because they were in his way. But sometimes, late on a winter's afternoon when mist is beginning to form in the valley, some slanting rays of late sunshine will strike those stones and the dead grass around them. For several minutes each stone will glow in the cold light of a winter sun. But then the sun will drop below the horizon and the light will be taken from the grove of stones, trees and the dead stalks of bracken at the bottom of the garden. And I find myself looking down there, and wondering.

CHAPTER 4

Vegetables

This chapter is entirely concerned with the growing of vegetables. The digging of the ground, the raking of the soil, the sowing of the seeds, the pulling of the weeds, the clobbering of the pests and the gathering of the harvest are all described here, but I am offering no advice. There are plenty of books and magazines giving advice on growing vegetables. Some contradict each other and some copy each other. Some advocate the good old methods; others pooh pooh them. This chapter tells how *we* do it and is not suggesting how you should. But we can proudly boast of modest success. We reckon to be largely self-sufficient in vegetables for most of the summer and autumn months but, come the end of November, we have to return humbly to the greengrocer we have deserted since May. By November we will have eaten the last potato, the tomatoes are running low and we know the carrots and beetroots won't last beyond the end of the year. But there will still be plenty in the garden coming along—the winter radishes, leeks and parsnips will take us through the winter. Then (frosts permitting) we should be picking turnip tops, kale and purple-sprouting broccoli. There is no time of the year that we can't go out in the garden and find *something* to eat. It is a very comfortable feeling. But it has meant a lot of hard work.

Having decided that the vegetable garden was to be the area over-looked by the kitchen window it was just a case of getting out there with a spade and start digging. We concentrated upon clearing and preparing small patches amongst the grass, and getting some seeds sown. When sowing things like, for example, leeks and brassicas, we just hoped that by the time they were ready for planting out we would have dug and prepared a bit more ground.

Our method of working was this: First of all we decided how long a bed should be then we removed the turf, a spadeful at a time, down the length of the bed. The turf was stacked neatly to one side, then the soil was dug out from the line, to the depth of about two spits, and this soil was heaped up out of the way. We now had a deep trench and we walked alongside it slicing off the next line of turf which was then put upside down in the base of the trench. This turf was then chopped up a bit in the trench bottom and we shovelled on top of it the soil previously removed, having first cleared it of stones and half bricks (which were piled up ready to take away as they might come in useful for path drainage) and the toothbrushes and broken clothes pegs, etc. (which were piled up to take away to the dustbin.) We then dug the soil from the ground just de-turfed and piled it upon the first lot (having removed all the rubbish as before). We kept going like this and ended up with a nice bed of roughly dug soil, with a trench one side (ready for the operation to continue as before) a neat stack of the first line of turfs removed and two large piles of stones and rubbish.

Alan was very good at this work. Bending almost double he would swing his spade, slice off a neat rectangle of turf, cast it to one side and then carry on down his line. He could work at ground preparation like this for about two hours and end up with a properly dug bed, all ready for the next operation. I wasn't so successful. I tried his bending-low-swinging-the-spade operation but either missed all together (and found myself trotting forward a few paces) or I hit the soil with a juddering thwack that brought the spade to a halt. So my method was first of all to mark out with my spade two parallel lines in the turf, then divide these lines into spade-sized chunks by making marks across the lines. (This was the easy bit.) I would then dig and lever up each turf (it usually came up as a 6ins. square lump), cast my spade aside and squat down, and with my hands pull off the soil, the stones and the rubbish, before moving on to the next lump. After about an hour of this I would probably remember something urgent in the kitchen that needed attending to, and abandon my ground-clearing effort for the day. But I was extremely good at making neat piles of stones and rubbish. So we soon decided that it was probably better if Alan did most of the de-turfing and digging, leaving me to gather up the stones and rubbish. Gradually, between the two of us, a few vegetable beds were prepared.

But you can't sow seeds into roughly chopped-up lumps of clay. Somehow we had to improve the soil within our vegetable beds and we did this by digging in sand, wood ashes, home-made compost and something we bought in a large sack called 'clay buster'. We had three tons of rotted cow manure delivered. It was dumped on the track in front of the house and we moved it by the barrow load to the back of the house. But, really, it was a bit too much too soon and we had no alternative but to pile it up on an area of lawn which we knew was going to be incorporated into the vegetable garden eventually. It was about 18 months before the last bit of manure was finally dug in. As a final topping to each bed Alan raked over a thin layer of commercial compost mixed with sand. This enabled him to make drills and sow the seeds into what we hoped was an acceptable medium for them. Once they had pushed through this it was up to them to make the best of what they found beneath. They thrived on it.

We are still digging sand into the soil and, depending upon the crop planned for a particular plot, the beds occasionally receive dressings of wood ash or lime. But we won't have any more cow manure delivered. Sometimes I take my bucket out into the forest and pick up some sheep droppings for the garden, and occasionally a friend brings us some chicken manure. But most of the soil improvement now is done with home-made compost.

Anybody can build scruffy, ramshackle, lumpy, badly-drained half rotted compost heaps; we've been doing it for years. We are perfectly aware of how compost *should* be made, but the siting of a compost heap and the type of construction best for the job are matters that require thought. Is it best that a permanent place should be made for compost heaps? Or should there be several heaps that you use in turn so that the nourishing ground beneath a used-up heap can then be turned into a vegetable bed? But while we dither over these decisions something has to be done with the buckets of vegetable peelings, coffee grounds and tea leaves that come from the kitchen every day. So a temporary site is agreed upon, and the bucket is emptied.

These slithery toppling mounds are not a complete disaster. They rot down eventually and, anyway, if they are levelled off and topped up with a bit of soil they serve as excellent beds for pumpkins and marrows. But now that we have decided upon permanent narrow beds in the vegetable garden, with permanent paths in between, we think it best that the compost heaps also should be maintained in permanent places. So, at the bottom of the vegetable garden, just in front of the main apple tree, Alan has constructed a 2ft. 6ins. square cage of 2ins. mesh steel, with removable sides, and in it we are now building a neat stack of compost. Everything compostable goes into that cage: all vegetable waste, garden trimmings, bracken, woollen cloth, grass cuttings and some weeds. Everything is cut or broken up into small pieces and the heap occasionally receives lacings of soot and lime. Sometimes, for good measure, Alan pees over it—a compost heap improving activity that is well known and approved off even by the Radio 4 Gardeners' Question Time team. I haven't yet tried adding my contribution. Soon Alan will be constructing another similar compost cage which will be sited alongside the other one and the plan is that we will always have one cage in use whilst the contents of the other one rot down. The nourishing drainings from each compost cage will seep down into the 'orchard'.

The first few vegetable beds that we dug out of the turf were in somewhat haphazard positions. Some went across the garden, parallel to the house; others went down the slope. At one time Alan made some terraced beds across the slope but gave up this idea when he saw the effect of rain on them in very wet weather. With the underlying soil being clay there was very poor drainage and the water collected in great puddles all over the beds. We now have just two small raised beds at the top of the garden, parallel to the house and near the back door (mostly for salad crops) but all the other beds run down the slope of the garden, with permanent paths running between. We maintain the paths by hoeing off the weeds and covering the paths with coal ashes from the sitting room fire. But sometimes the weeds push through again and we never seem to have enough ashes. However, during periods of heavy rain the water runs freely down the paths and doesn't sit around on the beds. The fact that picking the crops during wet weather is a downhill slithering exercise is something we are prepared to put up with.

VEGETABLES

Coping with the soil drainage on this soggy clay slope has been a problem right from the start. An almost level site had been bulldozed (amongst the rubbish tip spoil) for the house itself but a steep grassed slope was left in the front garden which ensured that all the water pouring down the slope in wet weather collected upon the paths (to join up with the water pouring off the roof). Being busy with other matters, it was nearly two years before Alan was able to do anything about this, during which time we were paddling about in large lakes of water every time it rained. Then one day he took his pickaxe and mattock into the front garden and started work. He dug out a narrow trench at the bottom of the slope and immediately adjacent to the path. Noting that the water was inclined to accumulate more on one side than the other, he helped it on its way, taking his channel around the side of the house and into the back garden. At one stage his gully passed between the path edge and a shed we had recently installed. As he planned to build a concrete slab and stone ramp leading from the lawn up to the shed door, he took his gully across the line of this ramp and into the slight ditch at the side of the garden. Now was the time to bring into use some of those tatty plastic downpipes. He laid them in his trench along the side of the house and across the lawn to the ditch. He then filled in over the top and got on with the job of building his ramp to the shed. The gully at the front of the house has been left open for the time being because we haven't yet decided how to shape the garden there. The first few buckets of water we chucked into the front trench to test the system proved that Alan had got his levels right. The water that was poured in at one end trickled dutifully out of the other end. Now when we have heavy rain it is most satisfying to see the water in the front trench flowing swiftly to the buried downpipe at the side of the house and then spewing out of the concealed pipe into the ditch. Since then, whenever Alan has constructed a level path across the slope he has used sawn-off bits of guttering downpipe to take the water away freely beneath the concrete slabs.

With the soil drainage being coped with and the soil improvement being maintained (and having come to terms with the fact that the growing season here is a short one) the only other problem in our vegetable garden has been unwelcome visitors—like cats, slugs and aphids of all colours. We deal with cats by hurling abuse and clods of earth at them and protecting all seed beds with wire netting. The slugs are either chopped in half with a spade or clobbered with a brick (an instant if somewhat revolting death) and the aphids are dealt with by a variety of methods. Blackfly on the broad beans has not been a major problem here and colonies of them on stem or leaf can be destroyed by squashing them where they are. Whitefly can be ignored (we get so little of it) but greyfly can be a real nuisance. A greyfly colony spreading over a crop of kale plants can almost destroy them.

Alan read somewhere that an effective crop spray could be made from a mixture of 1 part matured urine to 10 parts water so, for a while, he husbanded his resources in an old 1-gallon bottle in the shed. Now at this point I must be extremely careful what I say and I do not want you to think that in a furtive corner of his shed Alan has been concocting his own 'pissticide'. Oh goodness me no. He wouldn't do this because it is against the law. The Pesticide Regulations of 1986 have made it an offence to use any pesticide unless it has first been approved by the appropriate government ministry. So if you have been in the habit of throwing soapy water over your roses or spraying plants with your home-made brew of nettles or rhubarb, then you must stop it at once. If you persist in this illegal activity you could be taken to court and fined £2,000. In 1988 the Henry Doubleday Research Association queried these regulations with the Ministry of Agriculture, Fisheries and Food, and received confirmation from the then Head of Pesticides and Infestation Control Division that it was indeed an offence to use *any* home-made concoction as a pesticide. However, so far as I am aware at the time of writing, there are no regulations forbidding you to treat your plants to home-made doses of fertiliser or foliar feeds, and when Alan set off down the garden with his spray of noisome brew it was to give the kale plants an encouraging 'foliar feed' to help them in their battle with the greyfly. The effect was dramatic. Some of the greyfly appeared to have died on the spot and when we examined the plants the next day the flies that hadn't stayed put as brown corpses had rapidly taken themselves off. (Well, wouldn't you?) But we can't record continued success. When the rain washed off the 'foliar feed' the greyfly army returned and, after several further doses of it, the plants themselves were, understandably, looking rather fed up with the whole operation. Nervous readers may be reassured that Alan didn't spray any crop that we intended eating—only those plants from which we were hoping to collect seed. Fortunately the greyfly don't visit us every year in large numbers.

Removing caterpillars from the brassica plants is a non-stop summer job. In this household it is women's work and on any warm afternoon you are likely to find me in my sunhat out amongst the Brussels sprouts, kales and purple sprouting broccolis intent upon slaughter. I find myself talking to the plants as I bend over them, offering praise and reassurance as I fumble amongst the leaves and uttering triumphant expletives as a caterpillar is seized, dropped to the path and stepped on. But there are rules to this game of larvae hunting. When I see the cabbage white butterflies dancing over the crops I can only admire their skill, persistence and pretty flutters amongst the leaves. I cannot bring myself to chase and kill them. Even when a pair of butterflies locked together in passionate lust fall to struggle on the path at my feet I cannot bring myself to step on them. That wouldn't be cricket. Now if I can follow an egg-depositing large cabbage white butterfly down the garden path I can usually find her batch of eggs without difficulty. They are in little yellow clusters on the undersides of leaves and can instantly be squashed. But the small cabbage white is craftier. She drops off her eggs singly—one here, one there—and it's not easy to find them. Eggs that are missed turn into caterpillars that will get their come-uppance if I find them on my tours of inspection or if the great and blue tits find them on their daily round of the plants. Between the lot of us this pest can be controlled and we have never had a crop ruined because of caterpillars.

But when a caterpillar has eaten its fill of our plants it sets out upon the journey to find somewhere to pupate. We often find them walking up window panes—actually presenting themselves to us for immediate death. But sometimes the creature will win. Having survived crop inspections by me and the tits, this persistent creature sometimes finds its way across the garden and up the house wall to lodge itself underneath a window sill. There it will gradually turn into a neat dangling pupa which will hang suspended by a delicate thread until the time comes for it to hatch out into another butterfly to start the cabbage dance once again. If I find one such pupa I am in a dilemma. This creature deserves to live. I stand there undecided, looking at this vulnerable miracle of creation. I usually turn away and postpone the decision. Fortunately the crafty acrobatic tits have no such reservations. They regularly explore our window sills and take matters into their own beaks. Very few pupating butterflies survive hanging upside down beneath any exterior ledges.

The most dramatic looking pest was discovered as soon as we started removing turf from the garden. When I first found one I hadn't the faintest idea what I was looking at. There, nestling amongst the stones, earth and old toothbrushes was a very large, white curled-up larva with a chestnut brown head. If I had placed it upon a 50p piece it would have covered the coin. As I didn't know whether it was going to turn into something nice or nasty, I gave it the benefit of the doubt and carried it away to continue doing what-ever it had to do down in the rough. Then I found another, and another. Alan was digging them up too. In a square yard patch he unearthed 37 of them, varying in size from the jumbo 50p coin ones down to little things that could almost curl up on a 1p piece. We continued giving them the benefit of the doubt until we went indoors to have morning coffee and consulted the *Oxford Book of Insects*. We discovered that these creatures we had been handling with care and taking to places of safety were the larvae of the cockchafer—one of the most destructive pests in the garden and a menace to crop growing farmers. Cockchafers are very large, brown night-flying beetles that will come crashing into your windows if you have the light on during warm May or June evenings. If you have the window open they will zoom in and go blundering around the room like a demented conker and hitting objects with the sharp thwack of a bullet. Sometimes called May bugs, or June bugs, these beetles used to be quite common and I can remember once, when cycling at night, meeting one of them eye-to-eye. It was a painful experience.

There aren't so many cockchafers about now (except in our garden) and each time we slaughter one we feel slightly guilty about diminishing the numbers of these curious beetles, especially as we read that they are the principal food of the horseshoe bat. But if we want to grow vegetables then we dare not leave any cockchafer larvae in the soil. They have voracious appetites and they eat the roots of anything they happen to come across. We once had a dramatic demonstration of this in the lettuce bed. In the morning we had a line of sturdy little lettuces, many of them just about ready for me to start picking. In the afternoon of that day three of the lettuces had collapsed; their leaves lying flat in the mud. I investigated and found that I could lift the lettuces straight from the ground. They had no roots whatsoever. I got a trowel, dug into the soil and soon found the large lettuce-chewing happy cockchafer larva at work. We have read that these larvae live in the ground for three years, gradually turning into the handsome brown beetles with white 'dog-tooth' markings each side of the wing cases. We have dug them up as fully developed beetles ready to fly. And we slaughter the lot. But although we have now practically cleared them from the vegetable garden they are still with us—crashing into the windows on summer nights. So we are hopeful that plenty of them are living out their greedy lives under-neath the lawns and down in the rough, chewing away at the grass roots. And we hope we are maintaining a sufficiently large popula-tion of them to feed any horseshoe bat that happens to fly past.

We are constantly having to balance our needs against the needs of the creatures who share this plot of land with us. And this balancing act becomes rather tricky at seed-ripening time. We are quite happy for the chaffinches to eat *some* of our ripening kale or broccoli seed, but we don't want them to have *all* of it. So when we see them sitting in the plants happily munching away we have to cover the crop with old net curtains. And more old net curtains come out when we notice the jays eyeing the dangling pods of peas and beans. At the end of the summer the garden will have a multi-tude of plants left to go to seed, both in the flower garden and the vegetable patch, many of which have to be tied up with old canes and bits of string and some of them needing protection against the birds. It all looks thoroughly untidy but this doesn't matter because we know perfectly well that the only way to be sure of having viable seed for the next season is to save it ourselves. Even partially ripened damply gathered seed from this shady valley is likely to germinate more reliably than any seed ordered from a catalogue or bought from a shop.

We notice that the packets of seed we buy are always stamped on the back with a date indicating when the seed was packeted. Very interesting. It could have come out of the Ark; it could have been dug up from the pyramids; or possibly hanging about in some dusty warehouse since 1946; it could have been imported from the other side of the world and passed through so many hands that no-one knows *when* the crop was harvested. We are not to worry about such things. We are to be reassured that the seed was *packeted* last year.

Some years ago we were standing in a large ironmongers shop waiting to be dealt with about an order for wire netting. This shop had a revolving display stand of seed packets and I am guessing that the seed firm was responsible for keeping the stand fully stocked because there was a chap who looked like a salesman standing beside the stand and he was pulling out and re-arranging the packets. I noticed that he had a case full of seed packets with him and, as I watched, I saw him opening up seed packets from the display stand and emptying the contents into other packets he took from his case. The repacked seed was then replaced upon the stand.

Unfortunately we are not able to save the seed of many vegetables. (We have frequently tried, and failed, with parsnips and carrots, for example.) So every year we send off an order for seed or buy from a local shop, and if we get 50% germination of the seed we are grateful. Occasionally we have 100% failure. Furthermore we have sometimes found that the date is not the only misleading information on a packet of seed. We once sowed some seed from a packet labelled Sweet Marjoram. The germination seemed reasonable. But it wasn't sweet marjoram. It was green purslane. On another occasion we sowed (indoors, in a seed-compost filled container) a packet of Old English Lavender seed. Germination was not quite nil; we had one lavender seedling. But we also had several pale persicarias and a stinging nettle. Against this I must record the fact that we once bought a packet of thyme seed from a stand in a supermarket. Assuming that germination would be as dismal as usual, Alan sowed the seed thickly. But he thinks that every one germinated and we have been transplanting thyme seedlings ever since.

The point I am making is that buying seed is a chancy business. If you save your own you know where you are, and can expect 100% germination.

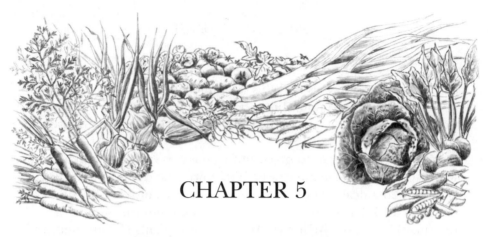

CHAPTER 5

More Vegetables

Every year, when sending off his seed orders, Alan will spend some time leafing through catalogues trying to find the particular variety of seed he wants. But he will also send for a few oddities—vegetables he has never tried before but that he would like to have a go at growing. And some of them are very odd indeed. Furthermore, he exchanges plants and seeds with other like-minded people who share his interest in horticultural curiosities. As a result of this you will occasionally find some very strange things growing in our garden.

Undaunted by the fact that we live in a shaded and frosty valley, he once attempted to grow some tiny marble-sized tubers called *solanum phurega* (better known as the golden potato) which apparently produces bumper crops of tasty potatoes in Spain, but I wouldn't recommend them to anyone else in the Forest of Dean. On receipt of the tubers in October, and carefully following the instructions, he planted each marble individually in pots of compost and put them in the back kitchen on top of the sink—a position which was cold but well lit. We had been warned that they would be difficult to store as they were disinclined to go dormant. You're telling us. Throughout the winter they put down roots and thrust up shoots, then perished. Leastways most of them did. Out of nineteen potted-up tubers only three survived and these were planted out at the end of March. Two of them gave up the ghost within a few weeks and the remaining tuber, which appeared to be growing strongly, was cherished. It was carefully protected against frost and it grew and grew and grew. It was, in fact, a damn nuisance. Its leafy wandering stems covered the bed and surrounding paths. It kept on flowering and it kept on growing. At the end of August came the time to harvest our crop of golden potatoes and this magnificent plant, which was now occupying the space that about eight to ten normal potato plants would need, yielded one handful (total weight 1 oz.) of tiny, marble-sized tubers.

Not so troublesome to grow, but yielding even less of a harvest, was an odd sort of cucumber which we understand is grown in Peru. With the botanical name of *cyclanthera pedata* (translated by Alan as pedal cycle) it has several common names the most pronounceable of which is a sneeze: Achocha. Alan grew two plants up wire netting fastened to the south-facing side of the shed where they romped away happily, finally getting tangled up with the Russian vine that was sprawling over the roof. The lime-green leaves and tiny flowers all looked very pretty and the bees seemed to like it. The plants produced 269 funny ocharina-shaped fruits, none longer than 3¼ins. and completely hollow. The bit I tried to nibble was tough and tasteless. The plants died in the first frost.

Hamburg parsley, claytonia and endive have been tried and found wanting. (Well, they certainly didn't want to live here.) But celtuce has grown sturdily and its crisp green leaves make an excellent lettuce substitute. The stems of this plant are supposed to be eaten like celery but we found them stringy and bitter. Par-cel is another reasonable success, so far. It grows like a very sturdy parsley and its leaves are celery flavoured. When I have been over-picking in the parsley bed (which happens frequently) it's useful to be able to find a few plants of par-cel that will serve as a parsley replacement. Now scorzonera is a curious vegetable with very long thin black-skinned roots and pretty yellow flowers that smell pleasantly like Birds Custard Powder. But the roots have no particular flavour, they are extremely fiddlesome to prepare and so we have stopped growing them. But we must have left some bits of scorzonera roots in the ground because it keeps on coming up. Never mind. The bees like the flowers. (Perhaps they too like the smell of Birds Custard Powder.) We have also grown salsify which is similar to scorzonera except that the roots are white skinned. It is equally troublesome to prepare, equally tasteless and so we don't grow it anymore.

It is perhaps within the *allium* family that Alan has carried out most of his trials, usually with great success, but he once grew a handsome-looking plant that he was told was called a Babbington leek. It looks nothing like a leek, grows like a garlic and the first time we tried it, tasted absolutely foul. We were both standing beside the sink when we first nibbled a raw bit and we both instantly spat it out. We tried cooking a few of the handsome things and, if anything, the flavour was even more disgusting. I was all for yanking the things out of the ground and composting them (or, better still, burning them) but Alan decided to leave some in the ground 'to see what happened'. What happened was that the things got fatter and fatter and over a period of about 18 months the bulbs grew from 1 inch diameter (which was the size they were when we first tried them) to huge bulbs with a circumference of about 11 inches. When he lifted one of them (because he wanted to plant something else there) he found it divided into two large bulbs which, when cleaned up, were snowy-white, solid and very attractive looking. He decided to risk another nibble, but stood alongside the sink, just in case. He found it had a mild and quite pleasant garlic flavour and we have been eating these bulbs raw and in stews ever since. He has now decided that this plant was wrongly identified to him as Babbington leek, that we had tried eating it much too soon after planting and that what we had was in fact an *allium* called Elephant garlic.

In my opinion the most successful line of plants we now have growing in the garden as a result of one of Alan's trials is the Good King Henry. This plant is a winner. It is perennial and provides us with a reasonable crop of sizeable and tasty green leaves right at that awkward time of the year at the end of summer and early autumn when I am in danger of over-picking the spinach beet, and the sprouts and kale are not yet ready.

But never mind the oddities. There are certain common-in-our-garden vegetables that we wouldn't want to be without. Here they are:

Artichokes (Jerusalem): This is not in fact an artichoke, neither does it come from Jerusalem, and there are a variety of explanations offered for its name—none of them very convincing. We love its earthy flavour in soups and stews. We also like them sliced and fried in deep fat or plain boiled and served with a cheese sauce. It has two main snags. One is that it can have a troublesome effect upon the digestive system and should never be eaten if you are expecting polite company, and the other snag is that the stalks grow very tall and sometimes, in high winds, they will blow down unless we tie the lot together and lash them to a handy anchorage. (In our case the apple tree or the cedar hedge.) Incredibly, some gardening books actually recommend growing artichokes to protect other crops from the wind. Such a recommendation is obviously put forward by people who have never actually grown the things but have read what other people have written on the subject and have misinterpreted the expression 'wind break'. We always save smooth tubers for replanting for the following year's crop and by doing this we are gradually improving the shape of the tubers we harvest. We now get fewer of those knobbly clusters that are such a nuisance to deal with in the kitchen.

Beans (Broad): Starting off with the well-known Imperial Green Longpod and Aqua Dulce Claudia seed, Alan has also sown Red-seeded Seville, Gloucester Bounty, Red Flowered and Martock beans—interesting old varieties, some with pretty pink flowers. As these were planted all in the same bed and the bees went dutifully from one to the other, the seed we saved for planting the following year turned out to be an interesting mixture, with flowers varying in colour from pure white, through mauve to deep crimson. Generally speaking, these old varieties produced a smaller bean and we can't say the flavour was any better. I wouldn't be surprised if one day Alan doesn't buy some more Imperial Green Longpod seed to sow in early spring, but in the meantime he is saving the largest pods from the strongest plants and producing a goodly crop of our own beans ('West Wonders'? 'Forest Favourites'?) that we have eaten fresh from the end of May to the beginning of September. Any beans left to dry that he doesn't want to keep for seed go into a large earthenware pot we keep in the kitchen and they are used up in winter soups, stews and savoury baked dishes.

Beans (runner and climbing French): Every year, in the sunniest and most sheltered spot in the garden, Alan erects a long structure of crossed-over canes up which he grows beans. He has been planting different varieties and types in groups along the line and I am not sure what goes on there because I am forbidden to go near it. He claims he is trying to find out which bean will give the best yield under our adverse conditions and he carefully picks and weighs the beans from his different plants each time I want some to prepare for dinner. He makes careful notes in his book (I see names like Rudolph, Liberty, Elizabeth, Purple Emperor and Pink Princess) from which he claims he will be able to make a decision as to the best beans for us to grow. I am not convinced. As the growing tendrils of Elizabeth, say, are quite liable to cross secretly to the pole occupied by the Purple Emperor, and her beans will dangle amongst his, how can he be sure what he is picking? And what about the seed he wishes to save for sowing next year? Although the bees will have buzzed along the row indiscriminately, Alan reckons he can tell when he opens the pod whether or not Rudolph has been interfering with the Pink Princess and the seed is carefully labelled and put away. But I don't think it matters. We are eating fresh beans, usually, from early September to early November and the leftover dried beans end up in the same earthenware kitchen pot as the broad beans. (The first year we were here we tried growing dwarf French beans—eleven varieties of them. But the slugs and snails had the lot.)

Beetroot: We have grown round varieties called Dragon and Devoy, and various Detroits, but we get on better with the long beetroot Cylindra. Our problem has been storing them in winter. 'Store in sand in a dry, frost-free shed' the books say. Who are these lucky people who have dry frost-free sheds? Our present sheds are new and were erected with care on good concrete bases (that's where most of the stones and half-bricks went) and they have been well and truly waterproofed. But a bucket of beetroot in sand last winter certainly became affected by frost in *our* shed. Next year we will have a bucket of them in the back kitchen and see how they fare.

Broccoli: We occasionally grow 9-star broccoli, but early and late purple sprouting broccoli is our standard broccoli crop. 9-star is a white broccoli which, in a good season, will produce mini-cauliflowers ranging in size from golf balls to cricket balls. The main central stalk flower head can be even larger and, if the plants grow well, we need only a couple of them to feed us with 'cauliflowers' throughout the early summer. (We once grew a 9-star broccoli plant that produced thirty-nine heads). But 9-star broccoli is not very hardy and we know we cannot rely upon getting a crop in this frosty valley. Even purple sprouting broccoli has a hard time here and, in a prolonged and severe frost, we can lose the lot. We save seed from our plants if we can. But if they have a late start and cannot produce seed to ripen by the autumn, or if they become badly affected by greyfly, then no seed can be gathered. Fortunately broccoli seed can remain viable for many years. (We have grown successful crops from eight year old seed.) So, as long as we gather plenty of seed during a good year we don't worry too much about the bad years.

Carrots: We have been getting unbelievably good results with carrots. We start pulling them when they are small, and we keep on pulling them until late autumn. We have grown incredibly large ones—some of them 9ins. long and with a top diameter of 2ins. I once lifted a monster of a carrot. I could tell by the part sticking up above the soil that it was going to be a big one, but when I heaved it out I found that it consisted of a bunch of seven roots, each one about 1 inch in diameter and joined at the top in a central hub measuring $2^{1}/_{2}$ins. across. I weighed the whole bunch. It was 1lb. 9oz. And the thing about these carrots—big and small—is their sweet, nutty, almost scented taste. They are orange all the way through and we eat them raw and cooked. They require no peeling or scraping. I just scrub them. And the name of this marvellous carrot? Autumn King. We have tried other varieties but Autumn King has been the best. Unfortunately we can't grow enough of them. With our short season we can make only the one sowing. Any still in the ground at the end of October will not grow much more and we haven't yet worked out a good way of keeping them in store. (See beetroot comments on our non-frost-free shed.) Last year, having read that Autumn King can withstand some frost, we decided to leave a couple of lines of them in the ground through November and December. It was a mistake. Certainly they seemed unaffected by frost but the slugs and other nasty nibblers got at them. I threw away more of the carrot than I was able to salvage. So, next year, any carrots left in the ground at the end of October will be lifted and stored in buckets of sand in the back kitchen.

Celery: Last year we tried the golden self-blanching summer celery. The plants grew very well and produced a forest of thin but tasty stalks. Unfortunately I think the slugs ate more than we did. We will probably try this again.

Kale: Possibly our most important crop. We prefer any sort of kale to any sort of cabbage because we can take just as many leaves as we require from the plants, and a few good kale plants will keep us supplied in greens for many months of the year. We can sometimes have a picking in late autumn but the main growth of leaves and flower shoots will appear the following April. We have tried ten varieties of kale but our favourite is Uncle Bert's purple. My Uncle Bert gave us a handful of this seed just after we were married and we have been growing it ever since. It produces purply-green leaves with ragged edges and leaflets sprouting out of the top surfaces of the main leaves, and we haven't any idea what its proper name is. We didn't think to ask. We accepted the seed from Uncle Bert with the casual unthinking attitude of all young people and it wasn't until we were middle-aged and Uncle Bert was long dead that we thought to wonder what the variety was. Had it been handed down, generation after generation, in my family? Or was it something that his next-door neighbour in Wiltshire had given him? We shall never know. We sometimes think it might be an old variety called Ragged Jack but having never seen Ragged Jack growing anywhere we can't be sure. But it doesn't matter. Uncle Bert's purple kale feeds us every year. Sometimes the plants collapse in hard frost, but they always recover, and sometimes they become badly affected by greyfly. Often the seeds don't develop and ripen, especially in hot dry summers but, like home-saved broccoli, our kale seed will remain viable for at least eight years. So, in a good year, we make sure of collecting plenty of seed.

Kohl Rabi: A curious vegetable, a bit like a turnip but it will grow in cold and wet conditions which, in our experience, a turnip won't. Under good conditions the kohl rabi will grow to a very large size but an old-fashioned gardening book of ours offers definite advice on this: 'to eat them when their flavour is best do not wait for them to grow to become the size of footballs', it cautions, 'but send them to the kitchen when they are no bigger than a cricket ball'. What our book didn't tell us was that the ideal ball-sized kohl rabi you bowl into the kitchen will not only be the size of a cricket ball—it will also be as hard as one. But, having sliced off the outside (with a sharp knife and a strong wrist) you will find the vegetable inside is sweet and nutty and makes a flavoursome addition to a hot pot.

Leeks: Musselburgh is our favourite leek. Some years we have grown others—Mammoth Pot and Lyon, for example—but we always return to Musselburghs because they have proved to be the most reliable. We usually start lifting leeks in November and the crop often lasts us until the following April. We always leave a couple of sturdy plants to go to seed, and on a warm summer's afternoon the charming pom-pom flower heads will be a-buzz with eager crawling bees. (Sometimes a drunken bumble bee will lodge itself between the floret stalks to sleep it off overnight.) Leek seed keeps very well. Alan once considered that some Musselburgh leek seed he had been keeping for seven years would no longer be much good so he chucked the lot on the compost heap. And a forest of unwanted leek seedlings appeared.

Lettuce: We always grow reddish-bronze lettuces (Salad Bowl, Redina and La Lollo Rossa) because we find that the slugs largely ignore them. Salad Bowl and Redina are prolific, albeit rather limp leafed, but La Lollo Rossa produces crisp little lettuces. We treat all our lettuces as loose-leaf types—i.e. picking odd leaves as and when required. We always try to save lettuce seed but have only been successful on a couple of occasions, with Salad Bowl and La Lollo Rossa, but the seeds have remained viable for six years.

Onions, including garlic and shallots: For salad onions we have grown White Lisbon, Guardsman, Japanese bunching and Red stemmed (autumn sown) but have rarely had any ready for pulling in the spring. We have Welsh onions and tree onions which increase rapidly but the bulbs and 'cocktail' onions produced are not very tasty. Minogues appear to be a variety of sand leek (rocambole) and are very useful in the autumn. We have lost our stocks of everlasting (non-flowering) salad onions but hope to obtain some more one day. With all these different clumps of onions growing around the garden, together with our chives and crow garlic in season, it works out that there is no month of the year that I cannot go out and pluck off a bit of onion flavoured greenery for use in salads, sandwiches and soups.

We keep ourselves in garlic and have done so for many years. (Our original stock were purple-skinned and came from Alan's mother who had been growing them since 1930.) The 'seed' cloves are planted in the first week of November and they are usually pushing through the soil by the end of the month. They aren't a bit bothered by severe winter weather and we forget all about them until the following July or August when the crop is lifted and left on a path to dry in the sun. This is the only part of the year we have to spend any time on the garlic. I bundle the crop into the shed overnight, or when rain is threatened, and eventually as the limp leaves start to wither I spend a couple of pleasant hours sitting on the lawn and plaiting the garlic into three or four long strings. I continue humping these in and out of the shed throughout the autumn, then they will be brought into the back kitchen and Alan will look them over and pull off a few choice bulbs, from which he will later select about 70 cloves for planting the following November. When the new crop is lifted I usually have a few somewhat withered bulbs left from the previous year's harvest and I throw these away in favour of the new juicily sticky bulbs that have just come out of the ground.

Shallots; we wouldn't be without them. We lost our original stock (which Alan's mother had grown from 1929) and so started again with some un-named ones bought from a greengrocer. The 'seed' bulbs are planted as soon as the weather starts to ease up after the winter and they grow without needing any attention until harvesting time at the end of July. They are dried off along with the garlic and they live in trays in the back kitchen—keeping us throughout the winter and spring with crunchy onion in salads and sandwiches. I also use them in soups and stews. Alan selects twenty or more of the best bulbs for planting the following year, and we eat our way through the rest. They will keep for more than a year—provided we have grown enough. We grow other multiplier onions, which are treated the same way as shallots. Iris Brander's potato onion has a milder but very pleasant taste, but Mrs Hutchinson's multiplier is exactly like a red-skinned shallot and exceedingly reliable. They have given us a good crop in years when, through prolonged dry weather, our shallot crop was rather poor. We don't know who Iris Brander and Mrs Hutchinson were—but they certainly knew their onions.

Parsnips: The most successful parsnip we have grown here is called The Student. Good tasty roots, mostly without blemish, we recently lifted a beauty weighing 2lb. 4oz. We have tried other parsnips including an old variety called Tender and True. Well, it was certainly neither tender nor true in our garden. The parsnips were small, tough, discoloured, multi-rooted and affected by canker to boot. Maybe they didn't like the patch of ground we gave them; maybe the weather was all wrong for parsnips the year we grew them. We don't really know, but from now on we shall probably stick to The Student.

Peas: When living in suburbia we didn't grow peas and so we had to start again with commercial seed. We started with Meteor because this seed produced excellent crops for us in North Wales but we found that the so-called Meteor seed we bought bore no resemblence to the seed we grew (and saved) in North Wales. This new seed was wrinkled instead of being smooth round. We have tried another variety called Little Marvel, which gave a very poor yield, an interesting 9ft. 6ins. tall pea called Purple Podded and some 7ft. high Ne Plus Extra which were a total failure. The Purple Podded pea looked very pretty, with its mauve flowers and mottled dark pods and, what's more, the birds weren't interested in them. The yield was very good but we found that they attracted a lot of attention from the pea moth. Moreover, the peas were tasteless. The pea with the best flavour and with the longest well-filled pods has been Hurst Greenshaft and this is the pea we will concentrate on in future. Needless to say, we save seed from the plants and I have no doubt we will be cropping a few odd West Wonders as the years go by.

Potatoes: When we lived in North Wales we reckoned to keep ourselves in potatoes from the end of summer until the late spring. Our favourite potatoes were Sharpes Express and Arran Pilot and any shapely potatoes of the right size were kept back for the following year's seed. But we also saved for seed any likely looking potatoes from the bags we bought from the greengrocer. More often than not we didn't know what sort of potatoes they were so we gave them names like Lloyd's Pink and Early Purples and we lifted some excellent crops from our home-saved seed. We grew no potatoes in our suburban garden but we wanted to start again when we moved here. So we decided to do the right thing and buy some Certified Scottish seed potatoes. We contacted a firm (who had been recommended to us by a prestigious organic gardening association) and sent for 7lb. of Sharpes Express. We posted our order at the end of the summer and hoped to receive our seed potatoes before Christmas so that we could lay them out for sprouting. But we couldn't. They arrived the following April and had to be put straight into the ground. As we didn't want to grow many plants we gave away two thirds of them: one third was planted in a well-tended garden in Bristol; one third was planted in a long-established and fertile garden in the Vale of Evesham, and one third was planted here. In none of these gardens did the plants prosper and in each case the crop lifted was poor and diseased. We didn't even trust ours to the compost heap. We burnt the lot on the garden bonfire. We have now gone back to saving seed from the greengrocer's bag and we are lifting good crops of potatoes once again.

Radish (Summer): We grow mostly Cherry Belle and French Breakfast and sprinkle the seed along the edge of any convenient bed. If the weather is suitable we make several sowings and we can be picking perfect little radishes throughout the summer. If the weather is not suitable we can have total failure. With coarse prickly leaves and scrawny woody roots, not even the slugs want them and they end up on the compost heap.

Radish (Winter): A most useful crop, giving us mild-flavoured radishes to crunch with our winter salads. We have tried three varieties—Black Spanish Long, Black Spanish Round and China Rose—but we have had most success with Black Spanish Long. In a good year we have lifted roots 9ins. long with diameters up to 2ins. and we are delighted that the slugs leave them alone. The roots are black-skinned, smooth, hard and fairly frost-free, although one year we thought we had lost the lot. That particular year our radishes grew so boisterously that two or three inches of each root protruded above the soil level and we found that during the winter frosts those parts of the root above ground were reduced to a jelly. However, when we lifted the crop (which appeared to be ruined) we found that each part of the root below the ground was in excellent condition. So we leave the crop in the ground and lift a radish when we want one. A slice of freshly-baked wholemeal bread, with butter, a hunk of Stilton cheese and a large piece of winter radish to nibble at is a favourite winter snack of mine (usually with a glass of white wine within reach) but I also cook these radishes. They can be plain boiled, like turnips, or added to soups.

Salading: To ensure that we always have plenty of raw greenstuff to eat we make annual sowings of Greek cress, green purslane, lambs' lettuce and wild rocket (which is almost the same as seed sold commercially as American land cress). We always allow a selection of plants to go to seed, and as I am sometimes a bit slow off the mark in collecting this seed the plants get plenty of opportunity to scatter seed of their own accord. Consequently we often get seedlings of Greek cress, purslane, lambs' lettuce and wild rocket appearing in places where they haven't been sown by us. Provided they are not crowding out another crop we let them stay. (I have gathered some of the lushest leaves of lambs' lettuce from plants that put themselves at the edge of paths.) Our original sowings of sorrel and salad burnet have now established themselves as reliable perennials, and we also find that some of the normally biennial wild rocket plants are annual or perennial. Needless to say, our summer salads are supplemented by leaves of nasturtium and the lushest of the garden weeds —details of which appear in the next chapter.

Seakale beet and spinach beet: We grow these vegetables alongside each other and although we reckon to allow only one of them to go to seed in any one year our seed has still produced some interesting beet crosses. But it doesn't matter. The vegetables are similar in growth and although perhaps the spinach beet is slightly more flavoursome I pick from them indiscriminately—enjoying the sturdy white stalks and dark green leaves of the seakale beet in the same dish as the pickings of spinach beet. They are both reliable vegetables, producing a thicket of large green leaves within a couple of months of the seed being sown in April. We pick from these plants until autumn when they are left for the winter. Sometimes the frost does nasty things to the edges of the leaves and the plants have to be stripped back and tidied up in the spring. But then they get going again and we can be picking green leaves from April until June, when the plants will start to go to seed. But by this time our sowing of the current year will be ready to pick. Slugs don't like them very much, butterflies seem to dump their eggs on the leaves only as a last resort and greyfly has never shown any interest. No wonder we love them.

Sprouts (Brussels): We think they *should* do well here but we have been rather slow in deciding upon a variety and allocating an appropriate bed for them. However, last year a friend gave us a handful of healthy little sprout plants he had left over so we shoved them in a line down the garden behind the herb hedge. They did very well and the eight plants kept us fed with sprouts from the end of September to the middle of December. The variety was Peer Gynt. Next year we hope to get organised on growing sprouts from seed but, as a matter of principle, we wish to avoid the F1 hybrids.

Squashes: We usually grow three or four bush marrow plants. In season I am picking courgettes almost daily from two of the plants but we let the other one or two plants produce marrows—some of which we leave to ripen for winter stores. We also grow pumpkins, usually two plants and we prefer the types that produce an abundance of small fruits. Once you cut into a pumpkin it must be used up within a fortnight, and a super-large pumpkin can become a weeping, mouldering messy embarrassment if you cut into it and leave it unused for any longer. The small bush variety called Golden Nugget produces a dozen or more pumpkins on each plant—each fruit measuring from 6ins. to 12ins. in diameter. They keep excellently throughout the winter in the back kitchen and I use them in flans, hot pots and soups, or just plain boiled or roasted. They have one snag. The outer skin becomes so hard in store that it needs a strong hand and a sharp knife to cut them up. We haven't yet tried using a hacksaw. It might be an idea. Needless to say, we would like to save our own seed from these squashes but if we are growing pumpkins and marrows together we daren't. We tried one year and although the seed we saved looked fat and healthy we found that germination was poor with the marrows and non-existent with the pumpkins. Moreover the marrow plants that survived didn't produce many courgettes and we were able to harvest only two marrows. There had obviously been cross pollination between the previous year's marrow and pumpkin flowers—to their mutual disadvantage.

Tomatoes: We like to grow one small variety (which just *has* to be Gardeners' Delight—no other tomato can match its taste) and one larger variety for slicing in sandwiches or cooking (including making chutney and sauce if the season closes-in on us). We have tried Outdoor Girl, Harbinger and others and may try one of the interesting-sounding yellow varieties. The only thing really consistent about our tomato growing is our insistence upon a few plants of Gardeners' Delight. But we have such a short season that we know our tomato growing must be done more in hope than in expectation. We start the seeds in pots in the kitchen but the plants are usually pleading to be let out long before conditions outside are warm enough for them. Nevertheless, we have never had total failure and we usually have tomatoes ripening in paper bags indoors during the autumn. Sometimes they last until Christmas.

Turnips: A very chancy crop. We usually sow a line of the variety Green Top Stone and if the spring weather is warm and moist we could be lifting, in the summer, nice little tennis-ball sized turnips with firm creamy insides. But quite often the weather is not warm and moist and we find ourselves yanking up a row of miserable twisted thimbles or bloated shapeless roots that have gone nasty inside. We usually make a second thick sowing of seed in late August to eat as turnip tops in the winter and early spring.

We find our vegetable garden a place of wonder and fascination. It is exciting to plunge your fork into the ground to lift the first haulm of potatoes. They come tumbling out as the fork is raised—potatoes large and small with clean unblemished skins. It is a delight to look at a dinner plate piled high with young carrots, peas, courgettes and tiny new potatoes—all of which were alive and growing just an hour or so ago. And it is satisfying to stand in the warmth of the kitchen on a dank November day, looking out of the window at the winter crops slumbering in the cold and wet ground. Against all the odds, our muddy patch is providing us with food.

CHAPTER 6

Herbs, Wild Foods and Weeds

I have yet to find a satisfactory definition of a herb. We have one dictionary which claims that a herb is a plant with no woody stem above ground (what about sage?), whilst another dictionary gives the definition: 'a plant producing shoots of only annual duration' (what about rosemary?). Most people accept that a herb is an aromatic culinary plant (what about borage?) and a book of herbal cures I was reading the other day was on about oak trees. I give up.

Weeds are equally difficult to define. I have read that the word 'weed' comes from the Anglo-Saxon word *weod* which means 'herb' or 'small plant'. So a weed is a herb is a plant is a weed. But here again I find that some other people do not share my confusion. A weed is any plant they don't like, or any plant which they suspect, however slightly, might be a wild plant, not a garden plant. We once knew someone who grew in her garden, and enjoyed, a whole bed of nettle-leaved bellflower. Then one day we pointed out to her that it was in fact a wild flower. She was horrified, and the following day dug it all out and burnt it.

Although definitions and plant classifications are of absorbing interest, we don't spend a lot of time pondering the subjects, nor do we come to many conclusions. Moreover, when browsing through dictionaries, botanical publications and seed catalogues, we note that the experts are not always in agreement with each other. We try to identify everything growing around us and can now put a name to most of the trees, shrubs, flowers and many grasses. Whether or not it is the *correct* name is beside the point. It doesn't matter. If it's beautiful, edible, useful or interesting, it can have a place in our garden.

Our herbs are growing everywhere. We have a small hedge of them curving down the garden between the lawn and the vegetable patch. We are keeping this hedge low, and at the end of the summer it is neatly clipped. Needless to say it carries on growing untidily, but at the second flowering we leave the seeding flower heads for visiting birds. We once watched a pair of goldfinches clambering happily amongst the heads of hyssop and lavender, whilst below them a secretive little dunnock neatly pecked up the seeds which fell to the ground. This hedge will be tidied up again in early spring. But individual herb plants are dotted about the garden, growing in situations which suit both them and us. Surely there can be no equal to a plant that pleases the eye during the spring, summer and autumn, and delights the nose and palate all year round? We grow various sages, rosemaries, marjorams, thymes and mints. We grow hyssop, parsley, fennel, winter savory and coriander. And all of these plants provide food for the butterflies, hoverflies, moths and bees as well as for us and the birds. Regretfully, basil will not grow out of doors here so we have to grow it in pots in the house.

We use herbs almost every day, either fresh or dried. A handful of fresh herbs will always be included in our summer salads and omelettes. We have them chopped in sandwiches, sprinkled over boiled vegetables and laid across joints of meat. When in May or June the plants are at their strongest I set about the task of drying herbs for use in autumn and winter. Ideally this job takes place just before the plants burst into flower and Alan combines the work of herb gathering with a bit of careful pruning and plant shaping. He will present me with several piles of mixed herbs to sort out and dry. This takes a lot of time. It is in fact a mammoth task which is often glossed over by writers of herb books and magazine articles. I have an arty-crafty cookery book which gives airy-fairy advice on the subject. There is a tasteful photograph showing a cottage kitchen table strewn with bunches of sage, thyme and marjoram (with no mention of the earwigs, woodlice and spiders probably lurking therein) and underneath the photograph there is the jolly suggestion 'Why not hang the herbs from the kitchen ceiling; they will look so attractive'. Not in my kitchen they won't. They will soon become covered with cobwebs and end up as so much shrivelled dusty vegetation that is fit only for the compost heap.

We wait for a sunny breezy day to do this herb-gathering job and I divide my herbs into small bundles, wash them thoroughly, drain them, and put them into muslin bags and hang them on the clothes line for a few hours. They are then brought indoors to finish drying in the bags until the leaves are crisp enough to be picked off and put into jars. Sitting at the kitchen table picking dried leaves off twigs and dropping them into pots is a mundane sort of peasant occupation which is an ideal thing to do when listening to a programme of music or a good radio play. But we love our dried herbs so much we don't begrudge the time spent harvesting them. We have them in soups, stews, omelettes, stuffings and all baked vegetable dishes. I am prepared to try herbs in almost anything—mint dumplings in pumpkin soup was a recent successful idea of mine—and it is a very comfortable feeling at the start of winter to know that we have an assortment of herbs in pots in the storecupboard.

We have several books on herbs and the information they give on their medical uses is most intriguing. It is nice to know that the parsley I am chewing will protect me against 'general weakness and tired blood' and that thyme is excellent if I am 'in travail' or my mind is 'disordered', but our personal experience of the medicinal qualities of herbs is extremely limited. I can thoroughly recommend an infusion of peppermint or watermint leaves as a pleasant hot drink to relieve a stuffy nose, and the next time you get stung with stinging nettles you will find that a handful of mint leaves (*any* sort of mint) will give instant relief. It's far more effective than dock leaves. But beyond that we cannot comment. We have had so few ailments we haven't put our herbs to many tests, and I suspect that if something really nasty ever afflicts us we shall abandon our ancient Herbals and seek help from the local doctor, like everyone else. However, if either of us finds, for example, that a disordered mind is giving us problems we will certainly go and commune with the thyme hedge. It's a bit nearer than the Health Centre for a start.

When the lavender and southernwood bushes are trimmed I gather all the bits, bag them up and hang them in wardrobes, lay them amongst jumpers, stuff them into the sock box and put them between sheets and pillow slips in the bedding chest. I'm not convinced that any of this keeps the moths away, but at least it makes everything smell nice.

At the end of each spring season when the garden plants are starting to grow strongly, I turf out all the old dried herbs from cupboards, drawers and pots and strew them around the garden between the vegetable beds. This is an optimistic gesture, done with the hopeful thought that their pungent aromatic scent will deter unwanted insects. I don't know whether it works or not, but the dried leaves might just as well be there as on the compost heap. We are not entirely sceptical about the powers of herbs—practical, medical or mystical—but we need to prove things for ourselves. Sympathetic or 'companion' planting is a theory that we have tried, but it hasn't worked for us. The idea is that certain plants placed alongside other certain plants, will send out various secretions or emanations which will work to their mutual benefit. We have also read that certain plants will protect other plants from insect attack. For example, sowing your carrots alongside a member of the onion family is supposed to deter carrot root fly. We can't say that we have noticed this. Sometimes we get the root fly; sometimes we don't— wherever the carrots are sown in the garden. And on the occasion that we grew shallots alongside the carrots the shallot leaves so swamped the struggling carrots they didn't develop much anyway. On the other hand, we have discovered that carrots grown amongst strawberry plants never suffered from root fly attack. It is all very inconclusive. Lavender planted around rose bushes is supposed to protect them from greenfly. Well, our greenfly didn't know this, and clambered happily amongst the rose twigs that protruded between the lavender stalks.

Yet there is one successful case of plants helping each other that I discovered quite by chance. We grow a small line of coriander each year because we like to harvest the ripe seed. We use a lot of coriander seed—in chutneys and sauces as well as in cakes, puddings and savoury dishes—and we have found that this is one of the few spices that we can grow successfully. But the fragile heads of coriander flowers end up being loaded with heavy ripening seeds and will collapse face downwards in the mud unless they are supported in some way. Last year we happened to sow a line of coriander adjacent to a row of parsley plants and I noticed that as the seeds formed on the coriander so the heads leaned sideways over the parsley. The parsley didn't mind at all. Eventually the whole line of ripening coriander seeds ended up being totally supported by the parsley and I was able to harvest an abundant clean crop of the seeds. In future we will always sow the coriander alongside a line of parsley.

According to our books parsley is supposed to be grown in a sunny, open position but we have found this plant to be marvellously tolerant of encroachment by other plants. We once sowed some parsley rather too close to a marrow bed. We had to leave our garden unattended for a couple of months and returned to find a thrusting tangled growth of trailing marrow plants, heavy with fruit, overhung with large leaves, and no sign of the parsley—until I started pulling off a few of the marrow leaves. There, underneath and completely covered by the marrow plants, was a bed of huge parsley. The plants were tall, with strong stalks and prolific with green leaves. As the summer had been exceptionally hot we can only assume that the marrow plant had afforded some much needed shelter to the parsley and prevented the ground from completely drying out. (Another case of 'sympathetic' planting?).

Such is our ignorance of many plants and our curiosity about them that nothing in the garden is destroyed without a good reason. Alan is ruthless with weeds in the vegetable seedbed (nothing must be allowed to interfere with food production) but once the vegetables are growing strongly and well able to look after themselves then the annual weeds will be left alone, with the exception of shepherd's purse which, we have read, harbours cabbage rootfly, flea beetle and other nasties. Only if a particular weed becomes too aggressive and is likely to swamp a neighbouring vegetable will it be yanked out. But there is nothing aggressive about the delightful little blue speedwells and scarlet pimpernels growing amongst the potatoes and I love to see them there. I also love the pungent smell of the ground ivy as I walk on it along a path between a flower border and a cedar hedge. Given half a chance the ground ivy will spread in all directions. It will crawl up the hedge and sprawl across the flower border so it has to be pulled out every now and then. But we would never consider getting rid of it all together. Another good reason for leaving some unaggressive weeds in the vegetable garden is that they will help to prevent the ground from drying out during drought conditions. Moreover, with any luck, visiting pests may choose to chew them instead of our vegetables. Presumably any cockchafer larva blundering about in the soil beneath our garlic plot would just as soon settle for a few daisy roots? These reasons alone are sufficient justification for leaving weeds in the garden but there is another one too. We eat them. Sturdy weeds are the first bit of fresh green salading to appear after the winter and there may still be some to pick in November, when the salad crops we sowed are becoming smaller, tougher and less tasty.

When the new growth starts surging in the spring I watch out for good weed specimens to earmark for eating. Dandelions that appear in the lawn are not worth picking. Through constant cutting their leaves will be too small but I can always find a few large plants growing at the edge of a flower bed or vegetable plot. Now dandelions could become a problem here. I love to see the bees crawling over them when they are in full bloom and the general plan is that the flowers are allowed to bloom happily, but are pulled off as soon as they go to seed. But we usually forget. Consequently we have rather too many dandelion plants in the garden. A few good examples of groundsel will be left for eating, and I can usually find some leaves of sorrel and comfrey from the plants growing down in the rough. But we can't, unfortunately, eat our way fast enough through the forest of goutweed which is steadily advancing upon the vegetable garden. We have read that goutweed was originally brought to this country by the Romans and was later cultivated in monastery gardens as a vegetable and a medicinal plant. They probably all regretted it. The plant is so invasive it will soon take over and smother all other plants. It can be eaten raw in salad or cooked like spinach, but we spend more time trying to destroy it than in eating it. We battle with it every year. So far we are on the winning side—just about.

Our stand of stinging nettles at the end of the garden behind the bottom oaks is really left as food for the butterfly larvae. But in early spring we eat some as well. With a pair of scissors (and wearing gloves) I snip off the tops of young nettles, wash them and cram them into a saucepan with a knob of butter. With a few minutes gentle simmering they soften to a dark green and are delicious, seasoned with a sprinkle of pepper and salt. But our favourite wild salad crop is chickweed. We leave plenty of it to grow wherever it happens to appear and we eat a lot of it almost every day, in season. With its soft green leaves and stems it is easy to pick and clean and we use it in salads, as a sandwich filling or just as a garnish. If left unchecked the plant could become a nuisance in the vegetable garden but it is easily pulled out of the ground when it starts sprawling too far.

At the end of summer when I am thinking about our winter stores we start looking with acquisitive eyes at the woodland around us. We have blackberries aplenty growing around our plot but we need to go further afield to gather rowanberries. Sitting at the kitchen table picking over a mound of rowanberries is another one of those mind-less peasant tasks that needs a good radio play to accompany it. A four-hour Radio 3 drama would just about cover the time needed to sort out seven pounds of rowanberries—which will produce about four pots of rowanberry jelly. When I think of the dreary labour involved in the making of these four pots—the picking, the washing, the boiling, the jelly-making, the four-hour Radio 3 play—I wonder at my dogged application to this job; that is, until I open the first pot in the winter. Then, as I taste and smell the initial spoonful of that exquisite jelly I know that it was worth all the suffering.

But it is not only berries that we're after when we set out for the woods with plastic carrier bags, it's fungi as well. People who know about these things are aware that out there in the countryside, growing alongside roadside verges and thrusting up through the woodland undergrowth, there is an abundance of delicious edible fungi just waiting to be gathered. People who are less knowledgeable on such matters (and that includes me and Alan) rely upon instinct, cautious enthusiasm and a well illustrated guide to mushrooms and toadstools to ensure that what is carried home in plastic bags is good to eat. We understand that most of the toadstools you see growing out there are worthless and it is not recommended that you eat them, but they won't actually kill you if you do. There aren't many deadly poisonous species. But we take no chances. When fungi-searching we go first thing in the morning; we gather only very fresh ones and, until recently, picked only the easily identifiable ones like field mushroom, horse mushroom, chanterelle and shaggy ink cap. But then we came across this beautiful toadstool standing 1ft. high in short grass on the edge of the wood. Its cap, measuring about 7ins. across, was a basic oatmeal colour with dark brown coarse scales over it. It was so clean and fresh looking that we just had to pick it to take home and identify. Sitting at the kitchen table with our specimen in front of us and *Collins Guide to Mushrooms and Toadstools* open at the appropriate page, there seemed to be no difficulties. What we had found was a parasol mushroom (*lepiota procera*) which was classified as 'edible and excellent'. An immediate decision was made to share it for breakfast so I cleaned it, cut it into several pieces, then cooked it in butter along with some scrambled egg and piled the mixture on toast. It was delicious; and we were out the next day with plastic bags to look for more.

Friends and relatives, knowing of our interest, are always happy to bring us specimens of fungi which they don't recognise. Offerings which they wouldn't dream of letting near their own cooking pots are given to us to 'try for lunch'. We usually have a go at identifying these gifts but rarely eat them. An essential part of the identification process is a knowledge of the exact growing conditions. We prefer to pick our own, and other people's gifts are usually discreetly composted. When it comes to eating wild fungi there is only one safe rule of thumb: When in doubt, chuck it out.

From time to time various groups of fungi crop up in the garden, and something dramatic appeared upon one of our bottom oak trees that had us worried for a while. Sticking out in plate-like layers from the base of the tree it was obviously a bracket fungus of some sort. Yellowish brown and oozing with little yellowish droplets, it looked positively evil. This time we consulted our copy of Roger Phillips' *Mushrooms and other fungi of Great Britain and Europe* and decided that we had a typical sample of *inonotus dryadeus* which was described as 'not edible'. (You're telling me.) We were somewhat alarmed to read that this fungus was a parasite of oak trees but were reassured by the comments of a local young man who is knowledgeable about such matters. *Inonotus dryadeus,* he told us, did no harm to the oak tree that hosted it. So there it stays. In the last couple of years it has become dark brown and as hard as rock. Occasionally it oozes globules of moisture. We shall continue to watch it with guarded interest.

The trouble with fungi is that many of the poisonous ones look innocent and harmless, whilst edible fungi can look rather unappetising. The death cap (*amanita phalloides*) probably looks quite attractive growing upon a woodland floor—we are judging by the pictures in our book, for we have never, to our knowledge, seen one—but it is the most deadly fungus known, whereas many of the boletus family—most of them 'edible and good'—look brown, squat and unappealing. We have something rather disgusting-looking which comes up in the garden occasionally beneath the birch tree in the back garden and also underneath the veronica bush near the front gate. We are pretty sure that it is the wood blewit (*lepista nuda*) which is described in our books as 'edible and excellent', but in colours of buff, brown and mauve—usually a bit slimy and slug nibbled—we have not yet been brave enough to try it.

In October and November we still take plastic bags with us on our woodland walks because following on after the berries and the fungi will be the nut gathering expeditions. To walk in the woods on a sunny October day is a delight which can only be described as 'uplifting', but I must confess that as we approach the magnificent stand of sweet chestnut trees greed takes over from reverence. Our eyes are not lifted to the canopy of golden leaves above but are searching the ground beneath. Are there any chestnuts here that the squirrels have overlooked? The English sweet chestnut is much smaller than the horse chestnut and grows within a protective fuzzy green casing which is covered with needle-like spines. To prise open these cases can be a very painful exercise and quite often, having stoically tackled this nasty job, you will find that the chestnuts inside are flat and unformed. The large number of opened and empty husks around the tree base tells us that the squirrels have got there first, and as they know what they are doing the chances are that any unopened cases will be worthless. But sometimes, if the crop is abundant, the squirrels are careless and amongst the prickly litter underneath the trees the rich polished gleam of fat chestnuts peeping from their cases will have us dropping to the ground and scrabbling about excitedly. We spend some time searching and prising and eventually carry home our harvest of chestnuts to roast on the fire. Each chestnut will be slit with a knife and we place a handful of them at a time in the roaster (a sort of long-handled frying pan with holes in it) which is then put in position over a suitable area of glowing fire. An occasional shuffle of the pan makes sure that they roast evenly and then the panful is tipped out onto some newspaper spread out on the hearth. With fingers still painful from the prickles we pick open the hot chestnuts, dip them in a saucer of salt and nibble away. We are usually on our knees in front of the fire at this stage. It's childish, delightful, tasty and great fun.

One year when there was a particularly heavy crop of chestnuts I put some aside to be eaten at the time of the winter solstice. This was not just a token acknowledgement of a pagan festival but also to see how well the chestnuts kept. Would it be worthwhile, on the occasion of a future bumper harvest, keeping some back for use in winter soups and stuffings, for example? Although the chestnuts we roasted over the fire on that winter solstice were enjoyable they were already showing signs of shrivelling. I don't think it would have been a good idea to try and keep them longer than the year end.

During the autumn months our two kitchens will look in a bigger muddle than usual. Paper bags of drying seeds clutter all surfaces; muslin bags of drying herbs dangle and boxes of shallots and strings of garlic have to be stepped over or walked around. Pumpkins and marrows are stacked in artistic piles on bench seat and table top, whilst boxes of apples are pushed underneath. Bottles of fruit and jars of jam, jelly, chutney and sauces will be filling my storecupboard. I can now sit back and enjoy that smug 'all is safely gathered in' feeling.

CHAPTER 7

The Pond

The older we get the more we realise how much there is that we don't know. When our curiosity is aroused about a subject we buy a reference book on it and only then do we start to appreciate the depth of our ignorance. But the trouble with opening a reference book is that you can immediately get side-tracked. I went to the shed one day to collect a trowel to dig out a large and unwanted dandelion and on the way back I had to pass the pond. I noticed a dragonfly that I didn't recognise zipping across the water, so I put the trowel down on the border and went indoors to look at our book on pond life. I identified my dragonfly as a common hawker and then I read on. Did you realise that the dragonfly nymph is the monster of the underwater pond life and that it not only waits motionless to seize in powerful jaws any other passing creature, but can also squirt its way along in a jet-propelled lunge after anything that takes its fancy? No? Neither did I. And I didn't know that the crafty caddis fly larva builds himself a protective little shack of sticks or stones to avoid such attacks. I spent some twenty minutes reading about that underwater jungle and then I went off and carried on with whatever it was I had been doing before I noticed the dandelion plant, and it was only the next day when I saw the trowel lying in the rain on the pond edge that I remembered it.

There was no pond here when we came but we knew that we were going to have to dig one. No garden is complete without water, be it a lake, a stream, an inlet, a spring or, as in our case, a large puddle. But we have never before had to give much thought to the matter of water in the garden. Our first plot of land had a spring which spurted from the hillside and ran in a chuckling stream down to a soggy pond. Alan made mini-waterfalls and little pools in ledges down the slope of the streamlet. He put a stone slab 'clapper bridge' across the water, building up his levels with stones and earth arranged in such a manner that something-or-other might find a useful hidey hole there. He planted bulbs and shrubs and trees and created sitting places for us. It wasn't necessary to do anything else to attract the wildlife. It just came. The frogs croaked at us from behind the stone rockery we built at the spring head; the tadpoles appeared in the pool amongst the water crowfoot plants and toads plodded about in the long grass at the water's edge. A water rat and a bad-tempered water shrew lived in the stream banks and lizards occasionally warmed themselves on the stones. They all got on with the business of living and breeding without any help from us. The pond was replenished by the spring water, and the annual cycle of growing, blooming and dying of the water plants carried on year after year as it had always done. All we had to do was watch, and enjoy it.

When we took over a small suburban garden between the A38 and the chemical works we planned no water garden. We put out a couple of frying pans which we kept topped up with water for resident and passing birds, and 'pond management' was just a case of chucking the water out and cleaning the pans when the oily film of diesel on the water surface became noticeable. And then I was offered some tadpoles from the primary school where I was employed at the time. We thought it might be an idea to introduce some frogs into the garden so Alan sunk a washing-up bowl into an area of shady border, put some rocks into the bowl as an escape route for froglets, and I carefully brought home, on the bus, an ice-cream carton (from the school kitchen) full of tadpoles. We knew that a plastic washing-up bowl full of tap water and stones was not an ideal tadpole habitat but reckoned it was somewhat better than a glass tank of tepid water in a hot classroom. The tadpoles thrived. I was feeding them (in accordance with the class teacher's instructions) on fish pellets bought from the pet shop, also bits of raw meat and fish. It was quite a pleasing experience to hold beneath the water a small lump of raw meat and have my finger and thumb surrounded by a pushing, nudging, sucking shoal of black wriggling little bodies. The tadpoles eventually turned into frogs which climbed up the stones and took themselves off into the garden where we hoped they were doing good works amongst the slugs in the flower borders and vegetable plot. Based on this experience I thought I now knew all there was to know about tadpoles.

The nearest water to our patch of land here in the forest is a stream about a quarter of a mile away, so as soon as we moved in we put out two bowls of water for the birds. These were to provide them with some drinking water whilst we gave thought to the pond we were going to have. Where was the best place for it? What shape should it be? How big? How deep? Having other things to think about, we dawdled over this decision until the need for urgent action was brought to our attention by a crow. He was standing beside one of the water bowls enjoying a drink then he stood for a moment looking into the water before pushing his face into it as far as he could, at the same time flapping his wings and flicking his tail feathers. That bird (whom we came to know personally) was longing for a bath. It was about time we provided him with appropriate facilities.

We decided that our pond must have shallow water at the edge to accommodate small birds, with deeper water in the middle for the large ones. It must be irregular in shape so that we could, in time, pretend that it was a natural feature. So we borrowed books from the library on How to Make a Pond; we bought gardening magazines running Special Water Garden articles, and we visited Water Garden Centres. It soon became clear to us that we didn't want the sort of pond that the library books, magazines and garden centres wanted us to have. We didn't want to stock our pond with fish. We didn't want to have to treat the water with 'Aquabright', 'Slime-erad', 'Bacteriascram' or any other chemical concoction to keep the water 'pure'. We didn't want any pumps, filters, fountain jets or spotlights. We just wanted an expanse of water in which the birds could drink and bathe safely and to which Other Interesting Things might be attracted. We wanted the pond to grow wild pond plants and to look after itself, more or less.

We knew that our pond would need some sort of lining. We weren't convinced that we could make a satisfactory job with concrete so we browsed through a water garden catalogue to see what was on offer. Plastic sheet pond liners carried a ten year guarantee, but rigid moulded plastic pond shapes were described as 'virtually indestructible'. As we didn't want to have to re-make our pond when we were in our eighties we decided upon a rigid shape and found exactly what we wanted in the catalogue. Measuring approximately 6ft. 6ins. x 4ft. 6ins. in an irregular but roughly triangular shape, it had a shallow but walled shelf all around the top, two slightly deeper shelves ocupied two angles, and the very middle of the pool was 22ins. deep. It was called a 'marsh pond' and we ordered one straight away. We decided to instal it at the top of the lawn immediately outside the sitting room window, and separated from the house by a small paved terrace. Alan dug an appropriately-shaped hole and when the pond arrived he bedded it into his hole with a good layer of sand. He tilted the pond slightly so that it would incline to overflow down the slope of the lawn. With stones he built up a small border around the pond edges, with an enlarged border at the overflow end to accomodate a 'bog garden'. He put a lining of pebbles in the narrow walled shelf at the pond top; he put some large slabs on lower shelves and he put two buckets of earth in the pond well. We connected up the hose pipe, turned on the water tap and filled the pool. It looked awful. It was a big sullen muddy puddle that took nearly a week to clear. But the birds weren't fussy.

We were now happy that the birds were provided for. We thought we could take our time over the stocking of the pond with plant life. We were wrong. If you provide the right habitat for a creature it will appear, and in our large puddle of water we had provided the ideal habitat for mosquitoes. They had the whole pond to themselves. There was nothing to prey on them. We were breeding thousands and thousands of them—little wriggling bodies doing yo-yo dances from the bottom of the pool to the surface. We were standing beside the pond with a friend when we first noticed them, and he suggested an immediate remedy. He reckoned that a squirt of Fairy washing up liquid would sort them out. The principle behind this, I gather, is that a detergent will destroy the surface tension of the water and the mosquito larvae could not hang on up there to breathe. Feeling guilty, in that I was about to commit murder, I prepared a bowl full of water well laced with washing up liquid and tipped the lot into the pond. It worked immediately. Soon there were thousands and thousands of tiny corpses floating on the pond surface. We then had the job of washing away all the detergenty water by leaving the hose pipe running and allowing the pond to overflow all down the lawn. We didn't think our birds wanted to bathe in Fairy liquid, let alone drink it.

Planting up the pond to try and create something resembling a natural pool of water was obviously an urgent job. We bought a water lily plant and sunk it into the mud in the pond centre. We set off into the woods with plastic shopping bags containing large plastic tubs and, from a pond and nearby ditches, we brought back duck weed, various pond weeds, water plantain, bits of things we couldn't iden- tify and some rushes, one of which to our delight turned out to be a reed mace. Most of this greenery settled down and made itself at home. The lily started to push up leaves and Interesting Things began to appear. The first were pond skaters, gliding over the surface of the water. Then we noticed the diving water beetles hurtling up and down. The time had come to introduce a few tadpoles. From the pond in the woods we brought back about forty of them. They were easy to catch (with a gravy strainer tied to the end of a bamboo cane) and they didn't have long to spend in the plastic tub full of pond water before they were tipped into our pond. There was plenty of cover for them beneath overhanging stones, general greenery and the lily pads, and I decided to give them a good feed. I scattered a liberal handful of fish pellets into the water. This tadpole-nourishing food was ignored. I saw them pushing past it with a total lack of interest. Now a tadpole wriggling through the water is surely one of the most daintily appealing movements it is possible to observe. But if they weren't going to eat the food I was supplying how could they survive? The tadpoles answered this worrying question of mine by lining up along the sides of the pool and grazing on the algae growing there. They seemed to be perfectly happy without any help from me. Is it only classroom-reared tadpoles that have depraved tastes and demand convenience food? Our reference books offer no advice on this point.

The tadpoles had a few more lessons to teach us. Those that survived the underwater predators and the above-water attentions of crows and blackbirds turned eventually into frogs and at least two newts. But we missed their intermediate development. The first we saw of the newts was two years after our introduction of tadpoles to the pond, when we saw two almost fully grown creatures swimming about beneath the water in between the lily stems, and occasionally shooting to the surface to breathe. This was late April and after a severe winter when the pond had been frozen over for several months. The frogs first came to our attention as fully formed tiny froglets leaping about near the pond edge. Some of these tiny but perfectly formed creatures leaped with such urgency and exuberance that they performed out‹of-control semi-somersaults in the air and landed facing the wrong way. We laughed aloud at their antics. This took place on a wet day in the autumn, just a few months following their introduction as tadpoles to the pond. We know we have at least a dozen toads in the garden but we can't be sure that they were born here. There is obviously a lot now going on in and around our pond that we don't know about—which is just as it should be.

With the stone-edged borders around the pond now growing, in season, crocuses, various stonecrops, saxifrages and aubretia, our pool area was beginning to look very pretty as well as interesting. And when the lily floated up several pink and golden blooms at the same time as the reed mace thrust its poker-like head into the air we had to stand and stare in admiration every time we passed the pond. But we have to interfere from time to time. The duck weed, which forms such pretty green plates of tiny leaves across the pond, could cover it completely and take out all light from the pool. The reed mace growth must be ripped out from time to time (we only have room for the one flower stalk) and the blanket weed must also be kept under control.

The underwater jungle life of our pond is a big mystery. We can't see what's going on down there but when Alan is clearing out some of the plant growth he sometimes pulls out lumpish creatures clinging to the undergrowth. He attempts to identify these lumps before putting them back into the water. Now you can't keep an underwater Thing lolling about on the palm of your hand whilst you go and get a reference book, so he tries to memorise its appearance and then, later in the day, he looks for it in one of our books. Needless to say, his identification is suspect although we can be pretty sure that most of the ugly lumps he dislodges are the nymphs of damselflies or dragonflies. That such unappealing creatures turn into dainty, colourful, fast-flying, gossamer-winged insects is yet another miracle of creation. The large red damselfly is with us all spring and summer and the first time we saw two of them joined together in tandem we weren't quite sure what was going on. Was he clinging to her backside or was she clinging to his backside? In which case how did they ...? Well, you see what I mean. Our reference book explained it all. The mating had already taken place and he was assisting her to deposit her eggs amongst the water plants. He would obligingly lower her to the water surface; she would eject her eggs and he would yank her back up again. Now there's husbandly co-operation for you. And you thought insects didn't care about each other.

Several species of dragonflies have similar reproductive arrangements. Our most frequent dragonfly visitor is one of the darter dragonflies called (we think) the common sympetrum, and he assists her to offload her eggs into the water but the whole operation is a much rougher affair. In fact the last time we watched this performance I got the firm impresion that it was all her idea and that he just wanted to be left alone to play around in the sunshine. They were skimming separately over the pond surface when they suddenly collapsed together onto the flower border with a clattering of wings. I can assure you that on a quiet summer's morning a pair of arguing darter dragonflies wrestling about on top of a cushion of saxifrage make a noticeable clatter. She finally fastened onto his tail and the two of them lumbered into the air together, gossamer wings shimmering in unison. But he didn't actually lower her; he appeared to be bashing her into the water and her backside was hitting the pond surface with a sharp plop. This went on for what seemed to be several minutes until he managed to shake her off and he flew to the side of the pond and rested upon a stone, poor chap. She continued bashing her ovipositor into the water, thus proving that she was quite capable of doing the job herself and had simply been attention seeking. According to our reference book this rough water-bashing activity was to wash the eggs from her abdomen so that they could sink freely into the water.

You can now perhaps understand why, on a warm summer's morning, our coffee break sitting upon the terrace beside the pond is such a long drawn out affair. If we move away from the pond we may miss something interesting. We once did. We noticed that one of the ugly lumps from the pond had crawled up out of the water and was clinging motionless to the side of the reed mace stalk. We knew that the miracle was about to happen. From this lump would emerge a damselfly or dragonfly. We guessed it would happen slowly over a few hours and so, at about half-hourly intervals, one or other of us would check the situation. Nothing happened all day. The following morning the lump was still there, so our pond watch became somewhat haphazard. By mid-afternoon I could see that the lump had changed shape somewhat and I should have stayed there watching. But I didn't. And when we next looked it had gone.

The insect life in and around the pond fascinates us throughout the spring, summer and autumn. But the birds are there all the year around. The amount of bathing that goes on during the coldest winter months astonishes us. Late on one winter's afternoon I watched a robin at the pool. The forest had been held in the grip of bitterly cold weather for many weeks. The soil in the garden was rock hard. The lawn was sparkling white with frost that never went away. Several times a day I had taken a kettle of hot water to a few shallow places in the pond so that a small area would be kept ice free but now, at the end of the day when the trees were silhouetted against a rapidly darkening sky, I could just make out the little shape of a robin at the pool. He was sitting in one of the ice holes up to his middle in water. He was splashing furiously, ducking his head and ruffling up his wings and tail. He then hopped out, gave himself a quick shake and then flew off to his roost in the cedar hedge where, with wet legs and feathers, he would spend the freezing night. I shuddered at the thought. But he presumably knew what he was doing. At all events, he was back on the doorstep the next morning demanding breakfast.

We have noticed that bathing in the pool is quite often a community affair with the birds. I wouldn't describe it as sociable behaviour because quite a lot of arguments take place, but it seems as if the sound and sight of one bird splashing about in the water will give others the same idea. One quiet morning at the end of summer we were watching a pair of bullfinches feeding from the green seed clusters on a tall straggly bulbous buttercup that was growing in the pond border. It looked a precarious operation. The slender stems of the buttercup dangled over the pool under the weight of the plump little birds who were bending forwards and neatly picking the seeds off. They were watched by a young bullfinch who was sitting at the pond edge obviously learning How to eat Buttercup seeds that Dangle over a Pond, and at the far end of the pool a pair of friendly blue tits were bathing together in a shallow corner. A young blackbird arrived, watched the tits for a moment, then obviously thought that bathing was a good idea so he jumped in and shoved them aside. They fluttered to another part and carried on bathing. By now a song thrush had arrived and then another and they joined in with the general splashing about. Then three more young blackbirds appeared and started to bathe, but were immediately chased by the first blackbird. They refused to go and ran around the pond edge to the other side. This blackbird chase carried on around the pool, the scurrying birds leaping over the thrushes (who ignored them) and underneath the dangling bullfinches. What had started as a peaceful summer's morning scene was now a splashy riot. The noise brought some great tits who came to see what was going on, and a quiet little dunnock who only wanted a drink was driven off by all the fuss.

Sometimes the birds will copy each other. We once saw a mistle thrush who was bathing, out of his depth, on a rocky ledge Alan had placed for the larger birds. But the mistle thrush wasn't bothered. He was making a tremendous splash, and ducking his head and neck right underneath the water. This activity was watched by another mistle thrush who cautiously stepped onto a rock at the other side of the pool and tried to imitate this head ducking activity. But her feet slipped and she gave a frightened flutter and scrambled out quickly. She ended up bathing primly in the shallow corner ledge, which we normally refer to as 'the babies' end'. Some birds are quite happy to bathe out of their depth—we have watched a song thrush bathing enthusiastically upon a slowly sinking lily leaf in the centre of the pool—whilst others are nervous of the whole affair and stand at the side doing little more than push their faces into the water and fluff out their totally dry feathers in a 'pretend bath' manner.

The crows now consider the deep rocky ledges to be theirs and they make a tremendous upheaval of water when bathing but they are the only large birds we have seen there. We have woodpeckers (both green and pied) in the garden but although they peck about on the lawn near the pond we have never seen any of them drink or bathe. Magpies, wood pigeons and collared doves drink at the pond but we have not seen them bathe. A jay once spent some time standing at the pond edge watching some redwings bathing. He had a rather puzzled look upon his face and for a moment it looked as though he might join in, but he just had a rather careful drink and then flew away.

We don't get many starlings in the garden but at nesting time a male starling often comes to help himself to some herbs, presumably for nest decoration. When we had a pair of resident starlings in a previous garden we noticed that most of the nest building was carried out by the female. On the rare occasions the male brought along some material (usually long dangling pieces of string or grass) she often chucked it aside contemptuously. So he usually spent his time sitting on the rainwater guttering chortling little songs of encouragement. But we think that the male starling that visits our garden here in springtime may have been sent by his mate to gather a few pretty bits and pieces to complete the nest decor. One morning we saw him running about jerkily amongst the cushions of saxifrage at the pondside, busily gathering a large beakful of flowers, when he suddenly stopped short and watched a blackbird having a splashy bath at the other end of the pond. Starling obviously thought this looked an interesting thing to do so he carefully laid aside his bundle of saxifrage and walked straight into the pond, found a suitable ledge and proceeded to bath noisily and splashily for several minutes. He then flew to the birch tree to flutter and preen, then he eventually flew off, forgetting all about his bundle of saxifrage left at the pond side. I wonder if he got told off when he got home?

The resident garden birds now take the facilities of the pond for granted and one or other of them will be at the water's edge almost every time we look out. The forest birds now know about it and will visit from time to time, and we are particularly delighted when we see the summer visitors there. That dainty little willow warbler (or was it a chiffchaff?) sipping the water neatly, that boisterous and showy redstart splashing away—were they the ones that came last year? And will they remember this pool in the forest when they come back next year? We like to think so.

CHAPTER 8

Birds in General

I should perhaps point out (in case you haven't noticed) that birds are an important part of our life. We cannot look upon them merely as interesting and charming objects to be observed and identified. They are individuals with definite personalities, some of whom we get to know very well. Note the pronoun there. We cannot refer to birds as 'things'; we give them names. Sometimes, if they are being destructive or a nuisance, we give them very bad names. One of the most destructive birds in the garden is the female blackbird. Given half a chance she will kick her way through a seed bed, pull out young plants, grab up chunks of saxifrage, and chuck all over the path the mulch you had just laid so neatly around a crop. She then has the audacity to come, with muddy beak, begging for food at the back door. I swear at her and flap a tea towel in her face.

In springtime many of the birds have destructive ideas. We once watched a pair of blue tits busily pulling to pieces all the carefully knotted bits of string at the top of our bean poles. Alan had spent a long time neatly tying all that string, and he now stood at the kitchen window, grim faced, watching the tits untie it all. To add insult to injury they were taking the bits of string to the nesting box Alan had recently made and fixed up for them on the side of the shed. In the hope of satisfying their need for string, yet saving his bean pole ties, he knotted a length of the same string to their box perch. He even teased it out a little for them. In their to‹ing and fro-ing of the box they stood upon this piece of string and occasionally looked at it. But they showed no interest. They had already decided which string they wanted, and they continued taking it.

Many of the birds like to take bits of the herb hedge for nesting material. Do they like the smell of it we wonder? Now that the hedge is established we don't mind this but when it had just been planted we had to protect a small golden thyme bush from the attentions of an energetic male starling who seemed to want to take the lot. A visiting collared dove, on the other hand, only wanted dead herb material. She wandered daintily about in the bed of winter savory, ignoring the young shoots of growth but busily breaking off dead stalks. She tossed these stalks about for a bit then carefully selected one long piece and flew off with it. She had taken a long time to make her decision and we were left wondering what it was about that particular stalk that had taken her fancy. Some of the birds choose odd materials for nest linings. The contents of the vacuum cleaner bag, for instance. Once when I emptied it upon the compost heap it attracted several pairs of jackdaws. Our resident sparrows, always happy to make do with whatever is available, will carry string and bits of paper up to their nesting sites under the roof tiles. All the birds seem to like hair. Having discovered that our own hair trimmings were taken speedily, Alan asked a friendly hairdresser for his floor sweepings. This bag of assorted clippings was emptied upon the compost heap but the hair didn't stay there long. Once again we noticed that the jackdaws took a good helping. In fact they took most of it, flying off with great wodges of hair sticking out from their overfilled beaks.

It is delightful to have birds nesting in the garden but it is also worrying. We know perfectly well that of all the thousands of birds born each year a lot of them have to die within a few weeks. It is the nature of things. But we would rather not face up to this fact. When the birds take themselves off to the woods to nest we don't know what perils they are facing. When they are nesting in the garden we feel partially responsible for their welfare and we worry about their safety. When we chopped the cedar hedge and put all the trimmings in a large pile down in the rough our resident blackbird (whose name is Bebe) decided that this toppling mound of loose branches was just the place for her nest. (She is stupid, as well as destructive.) We know that blackbirds sometimes make experimental mock-up nests before getting down to the serious business of building the nest proper so we didn't worry too much when we saw her carrying great dangling beakfuls of nesting material into the cedar pile. But she took a long time building this nest and then we noticed she was 'sitting' there—

in a nest no more than 2ft. above the ground and with an obvious entrance hole. We laid a piece of large-mesh wire netting across that side of the pile, hoping that we could thus keep any wandering cat at bay but we reckoned without the magpies. Magpies are persistent nest robbers. They will steal eggs and/or nestlings and it wasn't long before a couple of magpies started taking an interest in Bebe's nest. The noise of shrieking hysterical blackbirds would occasionally have me running to the back door and chasing down to the rough but the magpies just flew lazily up into The Oak and sat there cackling at me. They weren't bothered. They had plenty of time. And in the end they succeeded in getting at Bebe's nest and taking her eggs.

Bebe's second nest was in the *laurustinus* shrub in the front garden. At least this nesting site was more convenient for me (it is not far from the front door) but it is also alongside a fence. One day a cat walked along this fence and started working its way through the *laurustinus* branches towards the nest. Bebe's mate, Ben, is an attentive chap and normally spent the morning singing lustily from the house roof top but he now swooped down onto the fence and started shrieking for help. Bebe deserted the nest and flew to the lawn clucking hysterically. The great tits joined in with the general alarm and an agitated chaffinch called urgently from further along the fence. This cacophony of noise brought me running from the kitchen and into the garden. I reached the *laurustinus* just as the cat was stretching up one paw to the nest. I tried to sieze the cat; it tried to scramble down through the branches; I missed; it got away, and from a slightly damaged nest above, five blank-eyed faces looked down at me. I also noticed, much higher up in the top of the bush, the neat little cup of a chaffinch's nest that we didn't know had been built there. Bebe eventually reared those five young blackbirds successfully and they spent the summer being a nuisance in the garden chasing each other around the pond, fighting with other birds and tossing the mulch from off the vegetable garden beds and onto the paths.

We notice that generally the birds fight only with other birds of the same species, but when it comes to arguing over food we put out in the winter the biggest and bossiest will push the smaller and timid birds away. Robins fight each other all year round, whereas the quiet little dunnock fights with nobody. Once Ben and Bebe have got rid of their own brood they will allow no other blackbirds in the garden, but we notice that Bebe is especially nasty towards the song thrushes whom she will chase right from the garden. We have seen song thrushes chase only other song thrushes and we once noticed a song thrush and two mistle thrushes feeding peacefully together in the garden. It was March, when it might be thought that the birds were at their most aggressive, yet these three continued feeding in the garden together for about fifteen minutes, never more than a couple of feet apart. Perhaps they were on neutral territory.

Our birds acquire their names in a variety of ways. For example, Bebe was originally called 'Mrs Blackbird' which then became 'Mrs BB' which then became Bebe. This, of course, meant that her mate had to be called Ben. And if you don't understand the reference then you are a youngster below the age of fifty and didn't listen to the BBC Light Programme in the 1950s. A solitary coal tit who was with us during two winters became 'Coley' and another little tit who was either a marsh tit or a willow tit (we didn't know which) became known to us as 'Wish'. A visiting wood pigeon who was greedy for stale pearl barley we put out one winter became known as Pearl and she has remained 'Pearl' in spite of the fact we once saw her clumsily trying to mount another wood pigeon. In the middle of the lawn would you believe.

Generally speaking our birds keep their sex life to themselves, with the exception of our pair of sparrows who behave disgracefully on top of a cotoneaster bush, on and off (literally) all spring and summer. But we notice quite a bit of of saucy chase-me-around-the-herb-hedge activity, especially with the dunnocks and blackbirds. This catch-me-if-you-can performance between Ben and Bebe carries on all around the garden and always ends in what appears to be a squawking fluttering battle to the death, which leaves Bebe looking very crumpled and dishevelled. Once Ben has proved that he's the boss they get down to the serious business of nest building.

At the end of March and the beginning of April we start listening out for the real excitement of spring—the arrival of the birds who, for some reason known only to themselves, choose to fly in from foreign parts to nest in this country. The chiffchaff is the first to arrive, followed shortly after by the cuckoo. These two birds are the heralds of springtime and the first time we hear the cuckoo we exclaim to each other in delight, 'I've heard the cuckoo'. Those two repeated notes, pleasantly muted when heard across a distant meadow (not so pleasant when stridently shouted from a tree outside the bedroom window) will continue to delight us for a few days and then we get used to it and take it for granted. It's a pity that these heralds of spring can't sing very well. In fact they can't sing at all. The chiffchaff has a sweet little call but it's rather monotonous. No-one can enthuse much over a bird who has nothing to say except 'chiff' followed by 'chaff' and who keeps on saying this. Over and over again.

Then everything seems to happen at once. One of us will notice the swifts hurtling across the forest sky. The house martins will be busy plastering up their muddy cup on the gable end of a village house where they always nest, and swallows will be sitting on the wires outside the post office. The whitethroats will arrive, then the garden warblers and blackcaps and the whole woodland will be filled with song. But still we wait and wait, and worry until we hear it—the first song of the willow warbler. Every year this little bird seems to arrive later and later. And every year there are fewer of them. The first song of the willow warbler will stop us in our tracks. It is a poignant song, seemingly tinged with longing. It is a gentle cascade of rippling notes, starting quietly, as though the bird were unsure of himself and then getter louder and more hopeful, but dying away sadly at the end of the falling phrase. Last year it was the end of April before we heard it. We were walking in the woods alongside open heathland on a morning soft with sunshine and earthy scents and suddenly, as we stepped from the woodland onto the track, a willow warbler burst into song from the top of a hazel tree just above our heads. We stood and watched him. Seemingly oblivious to our presence this little bird with uplifted head sang his passionate song over and over again. We could see his open beak and his moving throat, so we crept away along the track. The nest was probably not far away from the hazel tree, and our presence may have been worrying him.

This trusting little bird chooses to make its nest just off the ground in long grass. A neatly woven domed construction of moss and bracken, it is at risk from marauding foxes, stoats, weasels, cats, predatory birds and, most of all, people. A happily stampeding family party, complete with children and dogs may charge through the woodland undergrowth or lark about on the heathland, all unaware that a short distance from their trampling feet is a fragile nest of eggs and a quiet little bird with frightened eyes. The willow warbler likes to nest in thinly wooded scrubland—rough sorts of places where gorse and bracken grow, with hazel, elder or hawthorn trees dotted about. Such lonely wastelands are now getting less and less and picnic parties will visit them most weekends. This is why we wait and worry each springtime until, once again, we hear that gentle song rippling from the woodland.

During the summer months the garden is bustling all day, from first light until dusk, with urgent and noisy birds. Parent blackbirds, tits, sparrows, chaffinches and greenfinches hurtle across the garden, beaks loaded with food. Visiting family parties of bullfinches, goldfinches and wagtails come to the pond, the youngsters all clamouring for attention. Greenfinch fledglings are particularly aggressive. We once watched Mrs Greenfinsh arrive with a beak full of goodies for her brood who were lined up along a birch branch. When she alighted beside them two of the fledglings jumped on top of her, squawking and scrabbling about on her head in their determination to be the one to receive food. The tits are reluctant to take food into their nesting boxes if they think we are watching. The blue tits will carry on feeding if we turn our backs and move a few paces away but the great tits want us right out of sight. One summer I was given the job of painting four l6ft. long pieces of 3ins. x lin. timber which were supported between two boxes on the lawn near the birch tree where, amongst the ivy, Alan had fixed up a box for the great tits. Painting my boards with primer was soon done, but by the time I got around to putting on the undercoat the next day the parent great tits were feeding the newly hatched youngsters and they absolutely refused to enter the box whilst I was standing on the lawn. I thought if I ignored them and carried on working they would get used to me, but they didn't. At one stage I had both parents sitting in the hedge just a few feet away from me. Both of them had beaks full of nasty-looking wriggling worms and crushed flies and they just sat there churring at me. 'Go ahead' I said, 'don't mind me'—but they did mind me, and I had to walk away with dripping paintbrush to enable them to enter the box. I had to keep on walking away from the lawn—every couple of minutes or two. It took me a long time to paint those boards.

When the summer weather gets too hot we stop work. We are always glad of an excuse to stop work, and the afternoon sun certainly beats mercilessly into this valley. We are then glad of our shady birch and oak trees. During that summer when we were putting up one of the sheds we had to start work at 7 a.m. because we knew we couldn't carry on after mid-morning. Alan's tools became too hot to handle. A spanner left lying on the path whilst he was assembling the nuts and bolts would become almost untouchable. But the trouble with sitting around in the shade thinking about nothing in particular is that you keep on seeing jobs around you that you should be attending to. On the other hand if you sit there long enough you can sometimes discover a valid reason for continuing to sit and do nothing. The marsh thistles growing down in the rough are a good example. I was sitting looking at them one summer's afternoon and had decided that it was about time I pulled them up. Even when in full flower, the scrawny, angular marsh thistle is no thing of beauty but now that the flowers were over and the seeding heads were about to take flight they really should be pulled out, I thought. And then a flock of goldfinches flew in. They settled upon the seeding thistle heads and twittered happily. I watched their bobbing black and red heads and their fluttering gold-banded wings. I saw the skilful way each bird trampled the fluffy thistle head so that the seeds were exposed for eating and I concluded that, on the whole, there's a lot to be said for sitting idly in the garden, thinking about nothing in particular. However, we have noticed that birds pottering about in the garden whilst we are out there will come much closer to us if we are in fact busy working. It is as if they reckon we are much too occupied with *our* affairs to notice what *they* are doing. Our resident robin, blackbirds and dunnocks will come within a few feet of our hands if we are out there on our knees weeding, but even birds unknown to us will ignore us if we are working and ignore them. From the kitchen window I once watched a pair of siskins drinking at the pond when Alan, about 14ft. away, was planting his shallots. He didn't know they were there and I knew I couldn't draw them to his attention without disturbing them. They both had a leisurely drink, pecked around on the lawn for a while and then flew off, whilst Alan continued working in the shallot bed.

One of the quintessential summer sights and sounds is that of a buzzard family party circling overhead. We stop what we are doing and look up. The buzzards have just one brood a year and when the family is taken for its first soaring flight they circle lazily overhead, their mewing cries getting fainter as they climb higher and higher into the sky over the forest. The buzzards are with us all year round but more often than not it will be a solitary buzzard that flies over the garden. During the nesting season any such buzzard will be pursued by a couple of hysterically raucous crows. But the buzzard shows no particular concern. He just occasionally flips a careless, arrogant wing at the pursuing bird and will slightly swerve to one side then slowly continue with his journey. When the buzzard family comes practising soaring over the garden then we know that summer is coming to an end and soon the swallows will be assembling on the wires outside the post office, getting ready for their flight south. Then, one day, we will realise that we haven't seen a swift for several days, and the house martin families are no longer swooping around the oak trees in pursuit of flies. Our summer visitors are leaving us. We think that the last to go are the willow warblers and chiffchaffs. We certainly hear them singing occasional songs well into October and we have seen one or other of them drinking at the pond during the same month. But we never know which it is. If they are not singing we can't tell them apart.

At the start of winter there is plenty for the birds to eat, in and around the garden. Small flocks of redwings will visit the old hawthorn tree outside the front garden fence and sit there chattering to each other as they gorge the berries. Blackbirds, song thrushes and mistle thrushes will feed from the berried bushes in the garden. Their squabbles are mild. Even Bebe will allow a song thrush to feed— provided she and the thrush are several bushes apart. Occasional fieldfares will visit the garden, and we once played host to a small group of redpolls who spent a long time pecking about daintily on the lawn beneath the birch tree, presumably feeding on birch seeds.

By the end of November we are usually getting bitter frosts and the berries will have all but disappeared. We then start feeding the birds. We hope they are glad of the food; we are certainly glad of the entertainment. We keep a nut cage filled with peanuts and this is hung from the corner of the front porch, just outside the kitchen window. Blue tits and great tits are the most persistent visitors to the feast, and occasionally a little coal tit will sneak in for a feed. A pair of marsh tits (or were they willow tits?) were feeding with us one winter, also a dainty pair of siskins who both showed nasty aggressive tempers if any other bird tried to push them aside. Sparrows and greenfinches, who are always with us jostle for room, but they will be sent packing when the nuthatch arrives. He clings to the cage face downwards and attacks the nuts with a ferocity that seems to threaten the wire mesh. Every now and then he will arch his back and look around, but if we stand still he doesn't seem to notice us just a few feet away the other side of the window pane. He has a smooth blue-grey back, an orange belly and a very smart eye stripe. He has a docile, smaller, mate who waits patiently on the porch roof while he feeds. He usually manages to extract a large piece of nut and he will fly off with it. She will then drop to the nut cage and feed. She never attempts to feed alongside him. She knows her place. But both nuthatches will be driven away when the pied woodpecker arrives, resplendent in his black and white jacket with bright red trimmings. He clings to the cage in an upright position and has a rather irritated expression on his face as though all this was really rather beneath him.

Birds who are unable to cling to the nut cage soon learn that rich pickings can be found on the path beneath the nut feast, and there will always be a few chaffinches, a dunnock, maybe a wagtail and a robin pecking about and clearing up the crumbs dropped by the untidy eaters above. I also throw out handfuls of wild bird seed on both lawns—back and front. This food (a mixture of seed, grain, pulses, nuts and stale pearl barley) is enjoyed by all the birds and has brought some surprising (to us) visitors to the garden. We once saw a female brambling feeding on the back lawn amongst the sparrows and chaffinches and on another occasion we saw a bird so brilliant, so startling and so unusual that at first I thought we were looking at an escaped exotic caged bird. In fact it used to be quite a common little bird but it has been so many years since we last saw one (about thirty years actually) that at first we failed to recognise it. There were a pair of them feeding on the wild bird seed, one with a brilliant yellow head with neat dark markings on it and a chestnut breast, and the other bird was similar but much duller. It was a pair of yellowhammers. They were with us for just that morning and we haven't seen them since. We don't often notice bullfinches taking food that I have scattered. They prefer to nip out young buds—forsythia, gooseberries, blackcurrants, quince—they aren't fussy. Show them a young bud and they will eat it. But they also like long-dead withered dried up old blackberry fruits. When we first saw a pair of bullfinches systematically working their way through the gooseberry bushes we thought we would have no fruit that year. We were wrong. The bushes were loaded with fruit. Indeed, if the bullfinches hadn't done a bit of thinning for us it was obvious that the bushes would have been overloaded. We have come to the conclusion that so long as there are plenty of gone-to-seed grasses, flowers and bushes around then the bullfinch won't do very much damage in the fruit garden.

Woodpigeons and jays seem to find plenty of food down in the rough. We have read that jays eat acorns whole, but how on earth they get them down and digest them we cannot understand. The woodpigeons move around down there in small flocks of about a dozen and rarely approach the house—with the exception of Pearl who has now come to expect a daily ration of wild bird seed. But she will allow no other woodpigeon anywhere near the lawn, the exception being that one occasion when lust seemed to take over from greed. If any of the flock of woodpigeons start to wander towards the lawn Pearl will fly at them with a ferocious clatter of wings. We are glad about this. We understand that woodpigeons can strip a vegetable garden of all green food within just a few hours. Even Pearl is not above reproach in this matter. She once started pecking at the turnip tops we were hoping to encourage into new spring growth, and on one occasion we had to drive her away from the kale plants. But normally she stays waddling about on the lawn looking for wild bird seed. We are hoping that if we keep her fed with enough of that she will leave our crops alone.

There is very little birdsong during the harshest winter months. Twittering parties of long-tailed tits sometimes visit the garden to swing in and around the overhead wires and the birch branches. In the woodland busily foraging little groups of goldcrests will chatter together in tiny high pitched voices, but only the robin will give an occasional phrase of song. Sometimes, on days that are silent with cold, a pair of ravens will fly overhead. They talk together, in companionable voices a 'kronk' from the one; a returning deep-voiced 'pruk pruk' from the other. And then one day, early in February, we hear the wild and lonely song of the mistle thrush, from his perch on the very top of The Oak. It is a song that carries far across the forest and we stop what we are doing to listen. We now know that winter will soon be over.

CHAPTER 9

Birds in Trouble

When a bird is ill or injured we feel helpless and inadequate. We have read of other people, neither helpless nor inadequate, who rescue injured birds, put splints on legs, bind up broken wings, wash oil-coated feathers, feed every hour with chopped up worms or milk through 'droppers', and release birds cured and repaired back into the wild again. Such people have our admiration and respect, but we cannot emulate them. We are terrified of doing the wrong thing and making matters worse. Many years ago, when driving in Wales, we came across an injured lapwing in the road. We stopped the car and I got out to go to that bird. With one fluttering wing—the other dragging—he scuttled away from me. I went after him. He went faster and finally turned off into a stubble field. So I left him. My instinct had been to pick him up, but if I had done so what was I going to do next? I didn't know. By chasing him down the road all I had done was to increase his misery and pain. Perhaps we should have left him there to be killed by the next passing car. I don't know. I remember the episode with guilt.

We hadn't been living here long before we realised that we were going to have problems with birds flying into the windows. The calamities have all been young birds, perhaps only just fledged. The first was a young green woodpecker who thudded into the sitting room windows and lay, presumably with broken neck, on the terrace by the pond. Shortly afterwards a young nuthatch did the same thing. Both were birds of outstanding beauty—even in death. We couldn't help stroking the soft feathers before we buried them.

One day I looked from the kitchen window and saw a young bullfinch sitting on the terrace. He was all bunched up and didn't look at all well, but an occasional blink of his eye indicated to us that he was not dead. A dirty mark on the sitting room window confirmed what we suspected—that he had flown into it. We decided to leave him there and watch to see what happened. Every ten minutes or so one of us would go to the window and check up on him. After about an hour we noticed that he was moving his head and looking around, but he remained squatting on the path. Another hour passed and it started to rain. The bullfinch stayed there, sitting in a puddle and getting wetter and wetter. I was now beginning to worry. We couldn't leave him there indefinitely—a prey to any passing cat. Perhaps I should go and pick him up, bring him indoors and put him in a cardboard box. I went out of the back door and slowly walked towards the bird. I made gentle reassuring noises as I approached. The bullfinch turned his head, looked at me with astonishment and then suddenly shot off, across the lawn and into the birch tree. I was so relieved that I swore at him.

This episode taught us a lesson; that any bird thudding into a window is likely to be killed instantly, or only stunned and, if left alone, may recover. Our tiny little coal tit once crashed into the kitchen front window. It was such a nasty cracking sound that we thought he could not possibly survive such a blow. When we looked out we saw that he was motionless, on his back and spreadeagled on the path. But we left him there, and when we next looked, about twenty minutes later, he had turned over. He was still sprawled on the path with his left wing sticking out awkwardly but he was the right way up. He stayed like this for about half an hour and then pulled himself together but remained on the path. When we next looked out he was sitting in the elder bush, about 20ft. away from the house. Before crashing into the window he had been jostling at the nut cage with other tits, but he now sat in the hedge with his back to the house, taking no interest in the nut cage. As I watched, he flew off into the woodland. But the next day a coal tit was back at the nuts, joining in with the general battle amongst the other birds. As there was only the one coal tit with us that winter we were convinced that this was in fact the bird who had been almost dead on the previous day.

More often than not the birds hit the windows with glancing blows and can fly away immediately, and of the ones who crashed head-on into the glass most of them seemed to recover, even a rather stupid thrush who did it twice on two consecutive days. She took longer to recover than other stunned birds we had watched. We noticed that for several days she seemed reluctant to fly and spent her time running about the garden feeding herself. (One night she roosted in a tall kale plant.) But when we eventually saw her fly up to the birch tree we considered that her troubles were over—for the time being.

Sometimes it is obvious that a bird in difficulties needs active help from us. Before we had the nut cage we used to fill a wide mesh plastic nut bag with nuts, and this was hung outside the kitchen window. One day a great tit got his foot entangled in the mesh and his struggles to release himself made the situation worse. I don't know how long he had been hanging by one leg and struggling before Alan noticed him and went to the rescue. Holding the bird in one hand he removed the nut bag from its hook and shouted for me to come and help disentangle the trapped foot. It was a difficult job. The thin filament of the mesh was tightly twisted around that tiny leg. I had to cut away the bag with scissors then gradually snip at bits of the stuff around his leg until I could prise it all off. All the time I was fiddling about, the bird lay perfectly still and silent in Alan's hand. There was no movement from the little leg that I was holding between finger and thumb whilst I worked. Finally I was satisfied that all bits were removed. The leg appeared to be undamaged and Alan went to the side of the garden and opened his hand. The great tit flew straight into the hedge and perched without any difficulty upon a twig. We have never used a flexible plastic mesh nut bag since that episode.

At nesting time the tits will investigate any likely looking hole. Slapdash workmen had left quite a few holes in the brickwork of this house and before Alan got around to filling them all in we noticed that two blue tits were carrying nesting material to a small hole halfway up the back wall of the house. At some time in the past some previous occupants of the house had decided that they wanted a shower cubicle upon the landing and the plumber involved had bashed a hole in the house wall through which to shove the drainage pipe. No attempt had been made to fill in the hole around the pipe. We hadn't at that stage decided whether or not we wanted to keep the shower cubicle on the landing so the pipe was still there, sticking out of the wall, and the blue tits were squeezing over the top of it, their beaks loaded with nesting material. Shortly after this Alan had occasion to do some work in the bathroom, which involved removing the bath side panel and it was whilst he was grovelling about on the floor that he noticed all the mossy nesting material bulging into the area underneath the landing floorboards. So it was obvious that the blue tits' nest was bridging the wall cavity. It was also obvious from the noise of squeaking coming from that mossy bundle that a brood of young blue tits had hatched. Over the next couple of weeks, when using the bathroom, we noticed that the tit family was becoming noisier. Soon they would be ready to fly from the nest and we hoped they could all squeeze successfully out over the top of that pipe. Well, perhaps some did but at least eleven didn't. We got up one morning to find six blue tits perched on various ledges in the bathroom, two fluttering about on the landing and one scrabbling about at the kitchen window downstairs. We managed, without much difficulty, to catch each protesting bundle of fluff and each bird was successfully launched into the back garden. But as I was pottering about in the kitchen preparing breakfast I realised that I could still hear the 'cheep cheep' of a young blue tit. And it was very close to my ear as I stood at the sink. There was a scrabbling and fluttering noise but there was no bird in the kitchen.

It didn't take us long to trace the source of the sound and to realise what had happened. Built into the kitchen wall was a venti-lator grille which lined up with a similar ventilator built into the brickwork of the outside wall. A blue tit had obviously fallen into the cavity between the walls and had fluttered along to the only source of light in that dark and dirty place. The bird was now clinging on somewhere between those two ventilators and waiting for someone to come and feed him. We couldn't see how we could help him, but we could perhaps help him to help himself. We removed the panel from the bath, thus allowing plenty of light to penetrate the cavity wall through all those plumbing holes up there, then we taped black plastic bin liners over both of the downstairs ventilators, thus cutting off all light to the blue tit. For a while we continued to hear the pathetic 'cheep cheep' from behind the ventilator and then there was a prolonged fluttering and scrabbling noise followed by silence. Later in the morning I found a dirty and dishevelled blue tit sitting on top of the bathroom cabinet and we congratulated ourselves on our successful rescue operation. Once we were satisfied that all baby blue tits had left the nest Alan trowelled a fillet of cement over and around that shower-room drainage pipe so that no bird would be tempted to use the hole again.

However, the following year there was a similar incident, this time involving a sparrow. The sparrows always build a nest under the roof tiles at the south-west corner of the house and the male sparrow seems to loaf around all summer, either on the guttering or atop the nearby cotoneaster bush, 'singing' in a penetrating and monotonous 'chirp chirp'. We understand that sparrows normally remain faithful to each other and their chosen nest site for life so it looks as though we are stuck with this pair whether we like it or not. On this particular day during the summer we were once again at breakfast when we heard a familiar 'chirp chirp' coming from behind the kitchen wall ventilator. How a fledgling sparrow had worked its way from the south-west eaves of the house through the cavity to the ventilator on the far west wall we couldn't imagine, but there he was, chirping away and demanding attention. We went through a routine similar to that of the blue tit rescue operation, but the sparrow (named 'Chirp', needless to say) stayed put behind the blacked-out ventilator and kept on, and on, and on. All day. We were irritated and worried and didn't know what to do next. Why was the bird being so stupid. Towards the end of the evening I realised that we hadn't heard Chirp for some time and I hoped he had now found his way upstairs to the bathroom. But he didn't turn up there. When I came downstairs the next day I reckoned that Chirp had either escaped by some other exit hole or was dead because we didn't think a fledgling bird could survive for twenty-four hours without food. We were wrong. No sooner had we started breakfast when that familiar 'chirp chirp' called to us reproachfully from behind the ventilator. Chirp's demands were loud and clear. 'Feed me, feed me'. Every time I went to the kitchen window or the back door I could see the worried looking parent sparrows, both with beaks full of dangling food, hopping about on the ground and looking up to the ventilator. Alan could stand it no longer. Fetching hammer and chisel he climbed up onto the draining board and bashed out the ventilator from the plastered wall. It came out in a few shattered lumps and revealed a U-shaped tray between the inside and outside ventilators. Upon this tray was an indignant but lively sparrow, and the tiny withered corpse of a blue tit. So either there had been two blue tits trapped previously and only one had escaped, or the dishevelled blue tit finally found in

91

the bathroom had not come from the ventilator cavity. We shall never know. However, Alan blocked up both ventilators, thus making sure that no light would attract any other cavity-wandering birds. He then replastered the kitchen wall. One day he might get around to re-decorating it.

We do our best to help any bird in difficulties but on one occasion I think we were responsible for causing distress to a pair of robins by encouraging them to nest in a box. We usually have two pairs of robins (a back garden pair and a front garden pair) who do a lot of singing and fighting but are always secretive about their nesting places. In early spring we see less of them in the garden (and we presume they are nesting somewhere in the woodland) but they visit most days to feed and to check up on what we are doing. Whatever job we are engaged upon in the garden, one of the robins has to come and supervise it. He will perch on the handle of a spade if you put it aside for a moment, or he will sit watching from the edge of the wheelbarrow. He will come within a few inches of your hands working in the soil and will graciously accept any small worms that are tossed his way.

The information in our reference books about robins' nests is a bit confusing. While it seems to be generally agreed that robins will nest almost anywhere—in holes, or containers, or sheds, or hedges, some books claim that the robin likes to be well hidden, whilst other books suggest that the hen bird likes an open side to the nest so that when sitting she can look out to see what is going on. In the Collins *Guide to British Birds* an illustration is given of a 'robin box' so Alan decided to make one. It was a sturdy cosy-looking affair and he fixed it high up in the cedar hedge, against a cedar trunk. Cedar foliage fell over the top of the box and it looked very inviting. For a couple of years no bird showed the slightest interest, but then one spring we noticed one of the robins carrying dead oak leaves into the box. We reckoned this was Babs—the books say that only the female robin will build the nest—whilst her mate Bob hung around in the birch tree singing encouraging songs to her. It was only then that it occurred to us that the box could be vulnerable to attack by a cat, so Alan constructed a large wire netting cage all around and over the box. This cage was firmly attached to the cedar trunk and 'ballooned' out over and around the box. No cat could get anywhere near the box, for the 'balloon' was too large and too wobbly. Babs sat in the birch tree watching Alan at work on her nesting site. As soon as he took his stepladder away she went to investigate. She seemed to approve and carried on taking oak leaves to the nest, sometimes perching on the wire netting on her way in or out of the box.

Building that nest took Babs a long time and she was being fussy about it. She appeared to be entirely filling the box with dead leaves, and then we noticed she was taking moss from the lawn and also some hair cuttings we had scattered on the flower border near the birch tree. When all this activity ceased we assumed that she was sitting, but we couldn't see her. She had completely filled in the front of her box with leaves and moss. In the meantime Bob sat in the birch tree and sang, and sang. But early one morning we noticed that Bob wasn't singing any more. In fact we could see no robins anywhere in the garden. I went to the nest and found that the wire cage was still intact but that mossy bedding had been pulled from the nest and lay hanging down in the hedge. On the ground were the remains of two smashed eggs. Later in the morning we saw both robins in the garden. They were obviously agitated. They snatched some food and flew silently off. We investigated the nest and found that the bedding was disturbed and there were no eggs there. As we understand that a robin normally lays up to nine eggs, and there were only two smashed ones on the ground, it appeared that something had stolen her eggs. No large bird could have got inside that wire cage. Something had climbed the cedar trunk. Could it have been a rat? Or is a plundering squirrel more likely to be the culprit? We shall probably never know. No nesting robin has shown any interest in the box since then, although we think it may be occasionally used as a roost.

Whilst we are prepared to go to the assistance of any bird in trouble, if it is fairly obvious what should be done, we feel particularly helpless and useless when faced with a bird who appears to be unwell but seems to have no visible injury. This doesn't happen very often. I presume that a sick bird usually takes himself off to a quiet corner to recover or die or be killed, but one winter we became aware that something was wrong with our dunnocks. Dunnocks are gentle little brown birds, with secretive habits and a pleasant rippling little song. We usually have three of them and they are always known to us as Tweedledum, Tweedledee and Auntie, although we can't tell them apart and, anyway, we have now learned that a consortium of three dunnocks is likely to be two males and a female. However, during that winter we first realised that something was wrong when we saw 'Auntie' behaving oddly one cold November afternoon. Fluffed up and looking woebegone, she was pecking around, eating and drinking a little, then she would hop away to find a corner on the ground out of the wind to rest. She appeared to doze for a while, then hop around again in search of food. As darkness closed in we worried about her. Should we catch her and bring her indoors for the night; or would it be unkind to scare her? As we watched she suddenly flew off, close to the ground and disappeared into the cedar hedge. So we stopped worrying. She was with us, moping about, for a few more days and then disappeared. A few weeks later we noticed Tweedledum and Tweedledee behaving in the same way and we decided to seek advice from the Royal Society for the Protection of Birds. We were astonished to learn that it was possible that our dunnocks had been infected with salmonella. Apparently outbreaks of salmonella have caused losses in wild birds reaching epidemic proportions over wide areas of England. Mouldy food and bird droppings were cited as being probable reservoirs of infection, and strict observance of cleanliness at all feeding stations was recommended.

As the food we give the birds is scattered over a wide area around the garden, back and front, we didn't think that bird droppings would be a problem, and the food never remains there long enough to become mouldy. But the birds certainly make a mess in the vicinity of the nut cage. We resolved to clean up after them more rigorously.

The sudden disappearance of the nut cage always causes astonishment and outrage amongst the regular customers. The nuthatches peer over the side of the porch, then shrug their smooth grey shoulders and fly away. The woodpecker looks more bad tempered than ever, but it is the blue tits who just don't believe it. They hover with rapid wing beats around the space where the nut cage used to hang, and it is several days before they give up trying to find it. But then, with urgent nesting business to attend to, most of the birds will leave the garden and take to the woods. We hope they have a successful season and that they will return, with their quarrelling families, to the feast which will be awaiting them outside our kitchen window the following winter.

CHAPTER 10

Birds in Particular

To gain the trust of a wild bird is an experience which is humbling as well as delightful. When we were living in a remote moorland cottage the birds treated us and our cottage as an interesting extension to their territory. They flew to our hands for food, they rapped at the window if we were slow in producing it and they hopped, walked or flew into the kitchen if we left the door open. With our nearest neighbour being a sheep farm a quarter of a mile away and the nearest hamlet with houses and gardens about two miles away, we didn't worry that these birds who trusted us would be at risk from other people and their pets. But here, in the forest, we are not living in a remote situation. The birds who come to our garden also visit other gardens. They are not *our* birds; they belong to the forest, so we decided that although we would probably give them names we would make no attempt to tame any of them. Unfortunately some of them have been successful in taming us.

Olive was a little chaffinch who used to come to the back door with a gang of her cronies begging for peanuts. I don't know why we called her Olive; it's just that the name seemed to suit her. Now chaffinches are quite noisy little birds. The song of the male chaffinch is a cheerful and noisy clattering trill and when he isn't singing he is often chatting away with a jolly and repetitive 'chink'. The female chaffinches also have quite a lot to say, but their 'chink' is a gentler sound and it seems slightly interrogative. It is more of a 'sweep?', 'sweep?'. When feeding birds at the back door the assembly of chaffinches was more or less the same each day—the males hovering in the background looking bossy and important but too nervous to come very close, and the females hopping about on the ground a few feet away from me. When a few peanuts were tossed out there would be a general scuffle, and each bird would fly off with a peanut in its beak, saying thank-you with a somewhat muffled 'peep'. But there was always one chaffinch left. I would be about to close the door when I would see, sitting patiently waiting on the path, a female chaffinch. We gave her the name of Olive and she became part of our daily life.

Olive obviously had problems. She was a perfectly formed little bird and could fly and hop about without difficulty but she didn't want to cope with the rough and tumble of life amongst the other chaffinches and she seemed to have no voice. She was totally silent. However, she soon learned that if she waited patiently for us to notice her, she would be fed. Once all the other birds had gone I would toss half a peanut towards her and she would hop to it quite slowly, pick it up and, usually, fly away with it to the hedge. But sometimes she would stay on the path and start to crumble the nut right there in front of me. I knew this meant that she was hungry and could she have a second one when she had finished this please? So I always waited until the last nut crumb had been eaten then I tossed her another bit which she would seize and take away.

This rather unhurried breakfast routine was soon noticed by a male sparrow. He would wait out of sight further along the path and when he saw the peanut come flipping out from the kitchen door he would suddenly swoop forward, grab the nut from the path and disappear into the hedge with it. In order to avoid these unpleasant interruptions Olive decided one day that she would like to be fed in the back kitchen please. She hopped up the step and came inside and looked up at me. I dropped a peanut to the floor and she sat there, between my feet, slowly crumbling the nut into little pieces and eating them. She then looked up for another peanut which she received and which she took away. As this was during the winter and it was often cold and wet, this routine of standing with the back door open whilst a chaffinch ate a leisurely breakfast on the lino was a bit of a chilly nuisance. But what can you do when a chaffinch looks up at you with appealing eyes? Sometimes the peanut that I dropped onto the floor bounced away from her and she would hop after it. She was obviously completely at ease. She was in no particular hurry and would sometimes sit there in front of the sink or by the table with her back to me, chewing up her peanut. She would then turn around and hop towards me for her second helping.

Olive seemed to spend all her time in and around the garden and if we were out there working she would hop silently up to us, so we got into the habit of always having a supply of peanuts in our pockets. We sometimes wondered if there was something wrong with her eyesight because if a peanut fell into the grass or down a crack in the soil she had difficulty in finding it and would come and silently ask for another one. But there was nothing wrong with her intelligence. She soon discovered that when indoors we spent most of our time in the kitchen, and if she hadn't seen us around the place for an hour or two she would fly to the kitchen window cill and peer in at us. And if we looked up from the dining room table and saw that sad little face then no matter how inconvenient we had to go and attend to her wants. We sometimes left a peanut for her on the window cill overnight so that she wouldn't bother us too early in the morning. But I think she really preferred personal service in the back kitchen.

At the end of winter the male chaffinches started practising their songs, the females started arguing with each other; there were a few up-and-down fights on the lawn and then they finally sorted themselves out and took off to the woods to nest. All except Olive. No-one wanted her. She was with us all through the summer and never liked to be very far away from us. She would follow Alan around the garden. But her silence was unnerving because if you didn't happen to see her you wouldn't know she was there. On more than one occasion I have been walking along the garden path, then suddenly realised I had forgotten something and turned around to walk back, only to discover Olive hopping along the path right behind me. She was frequently nearly stepped on. She wasn't always on the scrounge for food. We got the impression that she just liked to be near us. Sometimes on a sunny morning when we were sitting outside drinking our coffee she would come and join us. The three of us would be lined up on the terrace; Alan in his chair, me in mine and between us, squatting on the path, Olive would sit and doze in the sunshine. Sometimes she would potter about in the garden near us and we were pleased to see that she was able to find plenty of natural food, so she wasn't wholly dependent upon us and our peanuts. She was quite clever at catching flies that happened to pass her head.

During the autumn the chaffinch tribe returned to us from the woods and we were pleased to see that Olive became a little more assertive. After all, this was her personal territory. When peanuts were tossed out to an assembly of birds Olive would now join in with the scrummage. She never, so far as I can remember, actually grabbed a peanut from another bird but at least she was doing her share of pushing and jostling. However, she continued to expect her peanut on the window cill and the occasional breakfast in the back kitchen.

Amongst this latest flock of chaffinches there was another young female who drew herself to our attention by her non-stop querying call and the fact that she seemed to hang around with Olive. When Olive came hopping to the kitchen door, this other little chaffinch would follow behind. 'Me?' she called out, 'Me?'. If a peanut was tossed towards her she would approach cautiously, 'Me?' she asked. 'Yes, it's for you', I would reply. So we called her Mimi. When Olive came into the back kitchen Mimi would stay outside and continue expressing disbelief that the peanut thrown towards her was actually hers. 'Me?' she always asked. 'Yes, you', I always replied.

At the end of winter the songs and battles of the chaffinches told us that they would soon be leaving us and we noticed a slight change in Olive's behaviour. She still came to the back kitchen for her peanut but now she grabbed it and flew off, as though she hadn't time to bother with us; she had much more important things to attend to. She became more alert and less docile. Then one day she was about to hop into the kitchen when she stopped on the step, looked upwards above the doorway, then hopped back down onto the path. Still looking upwards she arched her back and quivered her tail. I poked my head out of the door and looked up. A male chaffinch who had been peering over the guttering took one look at me and flew off. Olive followed him. She went without peanut breakfast that day. Olive had something other than food on her mind.

She continued coming for occasional peanuts but she was spending more time now with the chaffinch flock. We hoped she would persuade her boyfriend to stay and nest in the garden but she didn't. When the flock took off for the woods Olive went with them. We never saw her again.

It is inevitable that some birds have personalities that appeal to us more than others. When our gloriously tuneful blackbird was turned out of the garden one spring by one that had no song to offer but two dull notes followed by a squawk, we were not pleased but could nothing about it. Nor could we do anything to help an appealing young robin that wanted to stay with us but who was perpetually chased off by another one who didn't appeal to us at all. We came to know both robins as speckled-breasted youngsters—one of which was furtive and kept out of sight most of the time, whilst the other was friendly, curious and spent so much time fidgeting around the back door that we gave it the name of 'Fidge'. We hoped that the two robins might be a pair and would eventually settle down with us, but this was not to be. When Fidge came close to us for food, Big Bully would come hurtling out of a bush and attack poor Fidge with a vicious fury. Sometimes Fidge would try to fight back, and the two birds would be a scratching, pecking feathery ball struggling upon the path, but the fight always ended with Fidge flying away.

Looking out for the birds that visit the garden is, of course, a non‹stop activity in this household. We chat to them if they aproach us and we mutter greetings if they are about their business in the hedge. If they are flying across the sky or soaring overhead we watch in silent admiration. This looking-out-for-the-birds activity continues even when the weather keeps us indoors, which means we spend a lot of time gazing from the windows.

It was when gazing out of the kitchen window one winter's morning that I first saw the common black carrion crow who, over the years, has become special rather than common and who has been given the name of Jo. Now a crow with its raucous voice and allegedly disreputable character is not normally regarded with much affection but Jo, with her glossy black plumage and smart feathery pantaloons, is very welcome here. We originally thought that this large black visitor to our garden was a male crow, but the bird's gentle dignity, intelligent eyes and cautious acceptance of us eventually persuaded us that we had a female crow here. (In our experience female birds seem to be more trusting than the males.) Each morning she plods carefully to the back door, her great black feet moving neatly around any plants in her way. She is very fond of cheese and pearl barley but her favourite foods seem to be raw meat, bread, pasta, cooked and chopped bacon rind and, of course, bones—which she holds to the ground with one foot. And she has this curious habit of dunking her food. Before we installed the pond she used to plod with a beak full of bread and bacon rind to the drinking bowl and drop the lot in. Bread which became waterlogged and sank to the bottom was retrieved with difficulty, the water sometimes getting into her eyes. Now that Jo has the pond at her disposal she no longer has this problem for Alan has arranged the slabs of stone so that Jo's dunked food remains readily available from the shallow water. When we first saw this dunking activity we thought that perhaps the bread was too hard or the bacon rind too salty but we notice that occasionally all kinds of food will be dunked and we have concluded that a crow sometimes likes to wash its food down with a gulp of water.

Jo's attitude to the smaller birds appears to be one of benign indifference. Tits, chaffinches and dunnocks will peck around on the grass within a foot or two of Jo's beak and she completely ignores them. But this is not the case with any other member of the crow family. Jackdaws and magpies hover warily at the edge of the lawn. Sometimes a magpie will try to sneak up and grab a piece of bread but Jo has only to turn her head and perhaps make a few strides of half-hearted aggression and the magpie will take off into the birch tree and sit there cackling. Once Jo has taken her fill of breakfast she will allow an approaching party of jackdaws to move up the lawn but she dives across their heads in a warning swoop as she takes off, just to show them who's boss. The jackdaws scatter obediently but are soon back to pick up the leavings.

Jo was with us for several weeks before we realised that she had a mate. We think he was probably sitting in The Oak watching her but was initially too nervous to join her on the lawn. When he eventually came to feed with her we were very pleased to see him and we gave him the name of Joseph. Joseph is larger and clumsier than Jo and it wasn't long before we realised that in Joseph we had a bird with a totally different personality. We have read that crows pair up for life. If this is so then we have every sympathy for Jo because she has the nastiest, greediest, most selfish, stupid, bad-tempered, neurotic, spiteful, suspicious, mean, avaricious and cowardly mate that ever a poor crow could be stuck with.

At first we felt sorry for him. He used to wait until Jo had landed to feed then he would fly to the bottom of the lawn and start walking up, in a jerky nervous way. If he saw us watching from the window he would immediately fly away, so we used to hide and peep out from behind the curtain. When Joseph eventually became brave enough to walk to the top of the lawn he would approach the food with a curious sideways crab-like movement then suddenly grab a piece of food, jump into the air with fright and drop it. He would again approach the food and go through this grabbing and leaping performance before he was brave enough to actually eat it. We wondered if perhaps at some time Joseph had tried to take food from a trap that had snapped shut in his face. We could think of no other reason for this behaviour. After a few months it seemed that Joseph was getting used to us. He would land to feed at almost the same time as Jo and he didn't mind us watching so long as we weren't too near. Even so, he still kept a nervous eye upon us and he was still inclined to grab at the food.

It was then that we started to notice his behaviour towards Jo. If Jo was quietly eating the food in front of her Joseph would decide that he wanted that particular bit of food and he would barge Jo out of the way. She never argued. She wandered slowly away to feed elsewhere, whereupon Joseph decided that he wanted *that* food as well. He would again push Jo aside and grab at the food. We partially solved this problem by setting out two or even three piles of food, separated by several feet of lawn. Jo still found herself shoved away by her greedy mate who, for a while, spent quite a lot of time running between the piles of food trying to prevent Jo from feeding, but at least there was always another pile of food for her to turn to.

Joseph was equally unpleasant at the pond side. If Jo decided she wanted to bathe and she stepped into the water to splash about on her slab, Joseph would decide that he too wanted to bathe, right there, and he would push her out of the way. Jo would patiently walk around to the other side of the pond but, more often than not, as soon as she started bathing Joseph would conclude that she had probably found a better spot to bathe in and he would insist, once again, on pushing her away from it.

We have never discovered exactly where the two birds roost but it is obvious that Joseph has the more comfortable spot. After a bitterly cold winter's night it is always Jo who appears in the morning with her back feathers coated white with frost. Joseph, always trim and black, obviously spends the night in a sheltered position. Does Jo perhaps crouch on the twig immediately over him? She is certainly a most attentive and loving bird to her brutish mate. We sometimes see them sitting close together in The Oak, Jo preening the back of Joseph's neck. She runs her beak through his feathers, lifting them in little bunches and then smoothing them down again. On one occasion when Joseph was unwell Jo's concern was obvious. Sitting together in The Oak, Joseph was squatting on a branch with his head held low. Jo kept looking at him intently and she occasionally smoothed his back with her beak. Joseph's head went lower and lower until it was between his legs. Then he suddenly opened his beak, gave a great heave and up came a gobbet of something large and probably nasty. It would seem that in his usual greedy way Joseph had gulped down somthing that on this occasion didn't agree with him. But all was well now. He sat up, pulled together his ruffled feathers and flew off, closely followed by Jo.

As nesting time approaches Jo spends more time preening Joseph's neck feathers and the two birds spend a lot of time sitting very close together. We know this because a lot of the cuddling takes place on the sloping roof of our large shed, which is within sight of the back kitchen window. The shed is built at right angles to the back of the garage and just a few feet away from it. By sitting together on the edge of the shed roof the two birds can stare at their reflections in the rather dirty window at the back of the garage, and this activity obviously fascinates them both.

We think that Jo was the first to discover the delights of that window. We saw her fly from the shed roof towards the window and she tried, unsuccessfully, to balance on the window cill. After that occasion we frequently saw the birds sitting together on the shed roof—Jo preening the back of Joseph's neck, and Joseph just sitting there looking at his reflection in the window glass and no doubt feeling very smug. Unfortunately, every time we went into the back kitchen we were seen by the birds and they immediately separated with embarrassment and started wandering around the shed roof. As soon as we left the back kitchen they got back to a serious bit of courting.

During these early days of courtship there is another change in their behaviour towards each other; a change which astonished us when we first observed it because it seemed to suggest that Joseph was not such a nasty bird as we had first thought. We saw him feeding Jo, but then we realised as we watched this little performance during the courtship season each year that it was part of a ritual and did not mean that Joseph was developing kindly feelings towards Jo. We came to know when this ritual feeding was about to take place. The two birds would be eating together on the lawn when Jo would stop pecking up food and would stand there with what I can only describe as a 'dopey' expression on her face. Joseph would then come bustling up to her with a beak full of food, whereupon Jo would open her beak and the food would be shoved in. Sometimes she ate it straightaway, sometimes she didn't. We once watched her take a beak full of food that Joseph had just given her and she hopped up onto the side of the pond and emptied it all out into the water in preparation for a pleasant dunking session. But no sooner had she off-loaded the food when Joseph came running up, barged her out of the way and ate it all himself.

They always build their nest in the top of one of the oak trees on the other side of the track in front of the house. We are never quite sure which tree they choose. The trunks of the trees are not far apart and the topmost boughs intermingle, so we don't know if they build a new nest each year or patch up the old one, but over a few weeks we see both birds carrying twigs to these trees. From then on, during the nesting season, we don't see so much of them. They occasionally come to feed but they spend very little time in the garden. We guess that Jo is sitting on the nest and that Joseph is not far away from her. Any buzzard, raven or other crow that comes too close to those tree tops will be chased off with a lot of energetic swooping and very loud cawing. One morning I heard a tremendous row going on in that piece of woodland. Looking out of the kitchen window I saw that a black cat was climbing up the trunk of one of the oak trees. There was no need for me to intervene. That cat didn't stand a chance. It had climbed about 8ft. up the trunk of the tree but was being dived at by a furiously flapping and shouting Joseph. Jo then joined in and the two birds constantly swooped at the cat, seeming to get within inches of the animal. The cat turned, dropped to the ground and then ran off, still pursued by the attacking birds.

We don't know when the eggs are hatched and we have never known how many young birds have been successfully fledged. They are never brought anywhere near the garden. I have occasionally seen one of the birds, at a distance in the woodland, feeding a demanding young crow and occasionally Jo and Joseph come to the garden to carry away food. We are amazed at the amount of food they can take. They appear to have a pouch inside their mouths underneath their beaks, and this is stuffed with food until it bulges. When the two birds return to their daily life of living in and around our garden they are alone. We presume that any young birds they have reared have now been ordered off the territory.

Jo likes to spend a lot of time sitting on the top of an electricity pole in the garden. Joseph sits on the top of a nearby tree. When Jo thinks it is about time they had some food she will fly to perch upon one of the electricity cables, in such a position that enables her to stare into the kitchen window. We usually respond by taking out some bread, cheese, pasta, grain or meat. She has trained us well. Invariably the food is dunked in the pond but quite often the birds will choose to bury some of it. I have seen Jo select a few choice pieces of pasta and then wander around the lawn or vegetable garden with it until she finds what she considers to be a suitable spot. She then makes a little hole, shoves the food into it, replaces the earth and then looks around for a suitable leaf or stone to mark the spot. They usually have no difficulty in finding what they have buried, but they don't find it all. When preparing a seed bed or lifting vegetables Alan sometimes comes across forgotten bits of bacon rind or a bone.

When throwing out fish heads or bones for them I usually toss out two, knowing that Jo will be down first to pick up one and then take it to The Oak to tackle the job of tearing it to pieces. Joseph will follow with the lump of fish or bone that she has left for him. But sometimes Jo, in an assertive mood will pick up both pieces and make off with them. Joseph will land upon the lawn, look quickly around and then fly furiously after Jo. If she has landed in The Oak we can see what happens. Joseph will march along the branch towards her and no doubt say a few harsh words. Jo always dutifully leaves one piece for him and then moves along the branch to eat her own bit.

We get the impression that Jo is much older than Joseph. Sometimes on a winter's morning when she flies into the garden from her chilly overnight roost she seems to be slow and awkward. There is a lot of stretching of wings and legs, and she occasionally stumbles. This is when Joseph is without mercy. He barges her away from the food and sometimes lunges at her with his beak. On a couple of occasions she has had trouble with one of her feet. It is obvious to us, when this happens, that she doesn't like to put much weight upon that foot but we can see nothing apparently wrong with it and the condition has improved as the days went by. Jo seems to be rather concerned about her feet. She spends quite some time paddling in the pond and we often see her looking down at her feet, first with one eye and then with the other. Is she wondering why they hurt? Is she getting a few twinges of old age? We watch and wonder.

On a recent occasion when her feet troubled her I felt obliged to go to her assistance when the birds came for breakfast. Joseph wouldn't let her come near the food. He not only pushed her but he pecked her savagely. Jo hobbled away and stood by the pond looking miserable. I went out with a handful of minced raw meat and tossed it onto the lawn. As I approached so Joseph moved away down the garden but he came running up when he saw the meat. Jo meantime came forward and started eating whilst I stood there. As Joseph approached the meat I wagged a finger at him and he scuttled backwards a few feet. He stayed there, dancing about with rage, whilst Jo carried on eating. When Jo eventually filled her beak and went to the pond to dunk it I stepped back and let the enraged Joseph come to the meat. He seemed torn between fury and greed. He didn't know whether to finish up the meat or to go and attack Jo. In the event greed took over and Jo was able to enjoy a long meaty drink at the pond whilst Joseph finished up the remains of the food.

At the end of the day Jo and Joseph usually sit together on the topmost twigs of The Oak. We often see them silhouetted against the sunset, but before nightfall they will suddenly fly off to their roost which is somewhere near their chosen nesting site. But occasionally, late on a winter's afternoon, Jo will decide to potter about on the lawn by herself. When the sun has set and the dusk is being overtaken by darkness, I sometimes see her as I draw the sitting room curtains. She takes off from the lawn, her great wings flapping skilfully beneath the boughs of The Oak, her long black legs trailing for the first few yards of flight. But on a winter's night the forest can be a bleak and bitter place for a weary old crow with troublesome feet, which is why we are always relieved to see her first thing in the morning plodding through the vegetable garden towards the back door.

CHAPTER 11

Butterflies and other Insects

Our sheds provide hibernation quarters for a large variety of insects. As the garden is surrounded by woodland, with many highly suitable over-wintering places, we wonder why these insects choose to pass their long sleep amongst the wellington boots, spades, forks, sacks, buckets and general junk contained in our sheds. Presumably they know what they are doing and they are certainly welcome to our humble facilities for as long as they like. But as soon as the first feeble rays of sunshine alight upon the shed windows they will be clamouring to get out. Latching open the shed doors ensures an exit route for most of them but there are those dim-witted individuals—notably lacewings—that flutter up and down against the window pane, apparently convinced that sheer dogged persistence will ensure their escape. The inside window ledges become filled with the dainty corpses of those who were proved wrong. As most species of lacewing are carnivorous and particularly enjoy feeding upon aphids, we would much rather they were outside in the garden searching for their favourite food in the brassica plot. But lacewings are fragile creatures. You cannot gather them by the handful and throw them out of the door. With finger and thumb each one must be grasped by the wings, carried to the door and released.

Sometimes on a sunny morning I am faced with a window full of these dancing fluttering creatures. I perhaps go to the shed in search of secateurs, string, a trowel or somesuch and then spend so much time removing lacewings that I either forget what I went there for, or decide that it's too late now and I go and make the coffee instead.

We have tried sticking black bin liners across the windows but this seems to have limited effect. The idiots prefer to line up and jostle each other in order to get at the slightest crack of light coming through the window rather than make for the great shaft of sunshine streaming through the doorway.

Our sheds also accommodate a few hibernating butterflies, usually some rather faded and tattered peacocks and tortoiseshells, and they too will emerge at the first hint of spring. They often pause awhile on the latched open door and display their wings to the sunshine. According to our reference book on the subject their first desire will be to 'pair'. We aren't convinced. Surely a good feed is the first requirement after a winter's sojourn in our shed? Unfortunately, at this time of the year there is little for them to eat in our garden. So I had this brilliant idea of remedying the situation by smearing a fingerful of honey upon the shed door. This ploy was an outstanding success and it is a very satisfying experience to watch a couple of weary-looking butterflies tucking into a feast of honey. However, I have since learned (from the Stratford-upon-Avon butterfly farm) that a 10% pure sugar solution would be a better meal to offer needy butterflies. If we insisted upon using honey it was suggested that it should be pure British honey as problems in foreign countries with the varroa mite meant the honey from abroad could be contaminated with a strong acaricide which is used to control these pests. However, we understand that the varroa mite is now infesting British hives too, so the purity of all British honey can no longer be depended upon. All in all, perhaps the 10% pure sugar solution is now the best option for hungry butterflies.

However, there are occasions when concern for a butterfly's future health is irrelevant. The injured ringlet with only one wing I found crawling about on the lawn one day wasn't going to live long anyway. I couldn't bring myself to kill it. I gave it some honey which was not only local, it was laced with whisky. I don't suppose this action did the butterfly any good at all; but it made me feel better.

Our concern that butterflies should have food and appropriate facilities to carry out their complicated life cycles means that flowers are left to bloom for as long as they are useful and that plenty of rough grass, nettles and bramble thickets are available. We have noticed that the chives are usually the earliest vegetable plants to bloom and they are very attractive to bees and butterflies. If we want to have plenty of chive leaves to eat we should really trim off the flower stalks, but we don't. The only answer is to plant more chives.

As summer progresses so we have the delight of butterflies all around us. Down in the rough the great arching boughs of The Oak have trailing branches that almost meet the common hogweed, this-tles and tall grass below. Over the tops of these seeding grasses the butterflies dance. They move so quickly and erratically that it is diffi-cult to identify them although we can guess what they are. Those cavorting little brownish/orangey butterflies are probably meadow browns, gatekeepers, small heaths and small coppers—all of which require the grasses as larval food plants. But the place to stand and stare at the butterflies is in front of a buddelia bush. There was one such bush in the garden when we came here; now we have them growing all around the place. Here we can watch the comings, goings and leisurely feeding of the red admirals, peacocks, painted ladies, commas and small tortoiseshells. All these butterflies require stinging nettles as larval food plants and we like to think that the butterflies feeding on our buddleia bushes make use of the stand of nettles at the end of the garden, beyond the bottom oak.

It was whilst we were standing in front of a buddleia bush one day during our first summer here that we saw a butterfly that we didn't recognise. It was as large as a peacock butterfly but it was bright orange with black markings. To see a butterfly that you haven't seen before is very exciting, and it doesn't matter if it turns out to be very common; if it's new to you, then the occasion is noteworthy, and it is at times like this that we grab the identification book from each other in our eagerness to give the butterfly a name. There was no problem on this occasion. Our new butterfly was a 'dark green fritil-lary'. Leastways that is what we decided then. But there is another similar butterfly called the 'high brown fritillary' which, according to our book, can only be distinguished from the dark green fritillary by some silver-pupilled red spots on the underside of the hindwing. As we can never get close enough to examine in detail their hind-wing red spots the true identity of these fritillaries must remain in doubt, and we are content to leave it so. The high brown fritillary is now extremely rare and has not been recently recorded in the Forest of Dean, so far as we are aware. If a few of them can make use of our garden they are most welcome. We subsequently noticed that our buddleia bushes were attracting a similar but larger butterfly that had iridescent green on the underside of the hindwings. This, we decided, was the silver washed fritillary.

Our identification of these fritillary butterflies may be questionable but that doesn't matter. What is truly exciting is that we seem to be providing exactly the right situation here for their continued survival. The high brown fritillary needs bracken to cling to; the silver washed fritillary needs to lay its eggs in the crevices of oak or birch, and the larvae of all the fritillaries need to feed upon violets. In this bracken-ringed plot of ours we have four oak trees and two birches growing and at the foot of the oaks we have some patches of violets. So long as we can maintain these conditions we can hope to have the joyous sight of those fast-flying fritillaries hurtling about the garden.

The numbers of our butterflies vary tremendously from year to year and we can never guess at the start of summer how many of which species of butterflies we are likely to see. Some years we seem to have a population 'explosion' of red admirals, yet the following year there may be few of them to be seen. We never seem to have many peacock butterfies—usually no more than five or six at any one time—but these numbers have, so far, been stable. There is no doubt that the commonest butterfly here is the small tortoiseshell. It is usually the first to appear in the spring and the last to disappear in the winter. They are all over the place all summer long. We have never tried counting them. We have no trouble counting the brimstones. If we are lucky we might see two or three of them right at the beginning of the season, along with the first tortoiseshells, but they rarely stop. We just see this flash of a large yellow butterfly dancing across the lawn and over the hedge. We wait and watch, hoping it will come back. Sometimes it does; sometimes it doesn't. It never seems to stop flying. But one year, at the end of March, a brimstone butterfly came to the front garden and stayed awhile feeding on a clump of prim-roses. Its wings matched exactly the colour of the primrose petals. That, for us, was a rare and delightful sight. Never before had we seen a brimstone butterfly settle to sun itself or feed.

Then we had the year of the painted lady. On one hot June morning we found the garden full of them—flying between the buddleia, the veronica bush and the marjoram. We were astounded

110

to read that these fragile creatures had flown in from North Africa. It so happened that this was also the year of the silver Y moth. They were all over the place having come, so we understand, from southern Europe. Did they latch on behind the contingent of north-flying painted ladies? Such mysteries of migration are beyond our comprehension. We are just delighted that these hungry travel-weary visitors can find refreshment in our garden. The silver Y moths were particularly pleased with our herb hedge. They moved between lavender, thyme, hyssop and marjoram on and off all day. They must have enjoyed a successful breeding season here because in September there appeared to be even more of them with us. And as they liked to 'roost' (if that's the right word) on odd bits of wood and stacked timber they were a bit of a nuisance. A silver Y moth perched on a rough oak bough cannot easily be seen. We probably inadvertently killed some of them. But we were very careful to remove the two that wanted to sleep on the underside of the wooden coal bunker lid that we were in the process of repairing. If you introduce an appropriately sized bit of twig to the forefeet of a dozy silver Y moth, and at the same time give it an encouraging shove from behind, you can get it to clamber aboard and it can be transferred to a place of safety. They seemed to settle down where I had placed them (underneath the timber pile) but they obviously preferred our coal bunker. They were back there the following day.

Trying to identify the visitors to our garden is great fun and wastes a lot of time. We were able to recognise the silver Y moth because of the little silvery marking on each forewing which could, with a bit of imagination, be compared with a sloppily written letter 'y'. But there are many little brown moths that are, well, just little brown moths and we rarely put a name to them. We have no difficulty with the large and dramatic ones (like the garden tiger and the privet hawk moth) and when one day I saw this large dark brown caterpillar galloping through the broad bean bed I knew that here we had the larva of one of the hawk moths. It was fat, about 3ins. long, appeared to be well fed and was most likely looking for somewhere to pupate. But if it carried on galloping across our vegetable garden it probably wouldn't last long. There were too many birds about. I tried putting it firstly underneath the forsythia bush and then at the base of the cedar hedge but on each occasion it turned around and carried on with its determined journey westwards. So I took it down to the rough and let it sort itself out down there. We had no problem identifying it as the larva of the small elephant hawkmoth but we were puzzled about its appearance in our garden. According to our book it feeds only on bedstraws. We have seen no bedstraws here and we have only recently started to introduce some willowherb. So we are equally puzzled at the occasional appearance of the humming bird hawk moth whose larvae also feed on bedstraws. This astonishing little moth is fascinating to watch as it does the rounds of our sage bushes. With its wings a blur of grey and orange it hovers in front of each bloom, its long tongue daintily probing each flower. According to our book this moth cannot successfully hibernate in Britain and it will either fly off to southern Europe at the end of the season, or perish. We hope that our sage bushes will provide it with enough nourishment for the long journey south.

Insects that come into the house are a nuisance. They can't possibly enjoy being indoors and we remove them as soon as we notice them. Butterflies are relatively easy to catch by hand—although a crafty small cabbage white once nipped in unnoticed and the feckless creature laid a clutch of eggs on a kitchen curtain—but we keep empty matchboxes in most rooms to enable us to catch the smaller insects. We had trouble one year with a persistent bush cricket that wanted to walk about on our bedroom ceiling. We were amazed to see it there. We thought that all bush crickets just hopped, like grasshoppers, and to get from our front garden up to the bedroom would be quite some jump. I caught it in a matchbox and put it out upon the front lawn but the following night it (or its friend) was back on our ceiling again. It was this repeated performance that enabled us to identify the creature. It was obviously an oak bush cricket, which is the only British bush cricket to live in trees and which can in fact fly. But we are unable to help the occasional lacewing that decides to hibernate in the house rather than in one of the sheds. The house is obviously not cold enough for these hibernating insects and they often spend the winter wandering about the ceilings upstairs. They walk from bedroom ceiling to landing ceiling and sometimes end up dead in the bathroom.

We go out of the way (quite literally) to avoid interfering with the butterflies in the garden. If a butterfly is sunning itself on a path then we avoid walking along that path. I once saw Alan with a wheel-barrow full of weeds suddenly stop halfway along a path, put his barrow down and come back to the house and sit on the back doorstep. He couldn't go any further, he explained, because a tortoiseshell was in the way. I too have been immobilised by butter-flies (usually tortoiseshells or peacocks) when they decide to come and sun themselves on my pinafore or blouse. I presume that it's the bright colours that attract them (I can't believe that it's my person-ality or smell) and if I happen to be drinking a cup of coffee I have to stop between sips in order not to disturb the thing. A handsome peacock butterfly once came and settled upon my shoulder. By slowly turning my head and squinting I was able to look him in the eye as he sat slowly opening and closing his wings just a few inches from my nose. And then I heard the telephone ringing in the house. Butterflies are more important than telephones so I continued sitting there for a couple of minutes until my colourful friend decided that it was time for another snack and he fluttered off past my face to the lavender bed. When the telephone caller eventually contacted me I apologised. 'I couldn't come to the 'phone before', I explained, 'because I had a peacock on my shoulder'.

On a warm sunny day there are so many bees, butterflies and moths feeding in the garden that although we may go out there with a sense of purpose to carry out a particular task, we find ourselves dawdling about. If we move too quickly we may miss something. This slowly meandering pace is particularly necessary along the path between the back door and the large shed. Here the rather lanky marjoram and snapdragon plants overhang the path and we have to wade through a rising cloud of fluttering and buzzing wings. We have disturbed these insects in their feast upon the flowers. They settle down again behind us as we pass along the path, but sometimes I have to just stand there and watch. There can be nothing more endearing than the sight of a bumble bee pushing its way into a snap-dragon flower. I find myself smiling as I watch its gradually disap-pearing backside.

If you start reading about the life-cycle of insects you will discover that some of them have habits that are not at all endearing. Some insects parasitise others by injecting their eggs into the body of the hapless host who dies slowly whilst nourishing the parasites within.

One day I was sitting in the front garden thinking idle thoughts when my attention was drawn to the path beside my seat by a furious buzzing sound. I looked down to see what appeared to be a small fluffy orange-tailed bee mounted on the back of a similar but all-black one who was resisting feebly. I had no idea whether I was witnessing an act of rape or parasitisation. Also I couldn't be sure whether I was looking at a pair of bees, hover flies or something similar. I picked off a bit of dried grass and tried to prise the struggling couple apart (in the interests of scientific investigation you understand) but my gentle probing was ignored. They were much too busy doing whatever it was they were doing, and the loud buzzing continued for what seemed like several minutes. Eventually the top insect released its grip and soared away across the lawn. The underneath insect sat on the path for a short while, pulling itself together, then it too zoomed off. On balance I think it was probably a pair of hover flies enjoying a bit of passion on the path, but I do not wish to enquire further. There are some things I would rather not know thank you.

Our efforts at identifying insects might be more useful if our memories were better. Every year we are visited by a couple of colourful beetles that we know we identified the previous year but whose names we can't remember. With the book now in front of me I can tell you that one is a wasp beetle and the other a variable longhorn. Both of them are harmless and handsome creatures that sit around on flowers sunning themselves. They seem to be in the garden for just a few weeks and then they disappear, until we see them back on flowers the following year by which time we will have forgotten what they are.

Ants are fascinating insects with complicated community lifestyles which we don't stop to examine when we find a nest in the vegetable garden. I apologise to them as I pour a kettle full of boiling water over a seething ant township, but they are interfering with our food production. A rapidly growing colony of ants can destroy an area of carefully nurtured seedlings. It's a case of Them against Us, and I'm the one with the boiling water. They can do what they like down in the rough or underneath the lawns but we won't have them in the vegetable garden. Well, that's the theory anyway. In fact they can be seen running around quite freely in the vegetable garden, and once a crop is growing I can't wade in with my boiling water. So we cannot claim to be victors in this Us against Them battle. One place in the vegetable garden where the ants in fact serve a purpose for us is in the broad bean plot. We are given to understand that ants like to feed upon the sweet secretions of blackfly, so when we notice ants running up and down the stems of broad bean plants we know that blackfly squashing time has arrived. But sometimes it seems that the ants are fooled. We frequently see them lingering hopefully over those little black spots you find on the leaves of broad beans. Or do the broad bean spots exude a sweetness too? The books don't tell us about this.

We sometimes have to rescue insects from the pond. I know that insect corpses floating on pond surfaces are all part of the rich pattern of living-and-dying pond life, but I can't just stand by and watch a struggling ladybird drown. I have to fish her out with a bit of leaf. But some struggling insects are beyond help. A damselfly arrived at the pond side once with fearfully damaged and shrivelled wings. It looked as though it had gone through a bonfire. Perhaps it had, and a bird had seized it and subsequently dropped it by the pond. I ended its struggles by stepping on it. But I was able to sort out the problems of a darter dragonfly that at first sight appeared to be in the same state as the damaged damselfly. The dragonfly was on a paving slab beside the pond and was obviously unable to fly. It kept on trying to get lift-off from the ground but each time it just turned a somersault. As I approached so its struggles became more urgent and the somer-saulting activity intensified. I soon saw what the trouble was. Two of its wings on one side of its body were stuck together and overlapping each other. I decided to have a go at separating the wings. The crea-ture couldn't fly as it was, so I was unlikely to make the situation worse. I squatted down on the path making reassuring noises and explaining that I was going to try and sort his problems out. The insect froze and remained quite motionless as my hands approached. It probably thought death was imminent. I took hold of each of the stuck-together wings, holding them between finger and thumb, and gently lifted one from the other. They came apart beautifully. The dragonfly remained there for a second, shivered its wings slightly and then suddenly shot off right in front of my nose and I saw it disap-pearing over the house roof. I was delighted with myself.

However, our benevolence to insects is not all-embracing. We have no affection for wasps in large quantities. Last summer we were particularly bothered with them and it was impossible to sit outside and enjoy a quiet glass of something. The wasps wanted to share it. They, too, are partial to a drop of beer, or wine, or sherry, or whisky. We tried giving them their own jam-jar of beer a short distance away but this meant that even more of their friends and relatives came to join the party. We were frequently driven indoors by them. A phlegmatic friend of ours once allowed a wasp to settle on her bare arm, assuring us that wasps did not sting unnecessarily and that if you just left the thing alone and didn't flap about it would simply take itself off. The next minute she was leaping from her chair with a yell and shouting for the Waspeze.

We are convinced that wasps *do* sting simply for the hell of it and we can't think of any useful purpose that they serve. This is why any queen wasp sleepily emerging out of hibernation in our shed will be immediately clobbered. We are prepared to put up with bush crickets in the bedroom, lacewings in the bathroom, spiders all over the house and egg-laying butterflies on the curtains but we will NOT (if we can help it) have any wasps queening it in our sheds.

CHAPTER 12

Beasts of the Wildwood

It is our custom early each morning to sit in bed drinking large cups of tea whilst we gaze out of the window at the woodland the other side of the track. In summer time when the bracken is high and the boughs of oak, birch and beech are hanging low and in full leaf we look out upon a scene of dense and waving greenery. But in winter time the woodland slope is brown with dead bracken and we are able to see through the leafless trees to the crest of the hill and the sky beyond. The scents and small sounds of woodland life come to us through the open window and we sit there peacefully drinking our tea and thinking those early morning meandering thoughts about life in general and the day ahead in particular.

I was sitting there quietly one spring morning, sipping my tea and wondering if it might be a good day to wash the bedspread when into my line of vision there wandered a young male fallow deer, his chestnut and cream dappled coat looking clean and new in the early morning light. He was only a few yards away from me, at the edge of the woodland beside the track and he paused and looked towards the house with a softly puzzled look upon his face. I was astounded— by his beauty, his daintily graceful walk and by the size of his antlers. I had never before seen a deer as close as this, nor one who was so at ease and obviously not in a hurry to go anywhere in particular. Alan was still dozing beside me so I kicked him awake and as he struggled to sit up so another fallow buck with a full spread of antlers wandered up and stood behind his brother looking across to the house. But they soon became bored with gazing at us and they slowly turned and walked up the slope, nosing into the bracken every now and then.

We watched until they reached the top of the hill. They then trotted out of sight. We have read that fallow deer were introduced to the Forest of Dean by the Normans (presumably to keep the king's hunting chase well stocked) and that they have been here ever since.

We also share the forest with badgers and adders but we have seen nothing of either creature. To watch a family of badger cubs playing near the set at dusk must be a delightful experience. I'm not too sure about the delights of watching adders—except at a safe distance. We understand that on sunny afternoons it is quite possible to come across an adder curled up and enjoying a bask in the warmth, and we are always on the look-out for them when we are walking in the woods. If an adder hears you approach it will slither quickly out of the way; it desires a confrontation no more than you do. It is only if you accidentally step on it that you are likely to be bitten—or so we have read.

There is a Forest of Dean legend concerning a strange and malevolent wild beast roaming the woodlands. Such a legend is probably inevitable in such a place as this. Every now and then the local newspapers will carry reports of someone's sighting of this creature, usually described as cat-like but about the size of a puma. The colour claimed for the beast varies from black to dark grey and the newspapers occasionally print fuzzy photographs of a distant streaking animal or a close-up of footprints in the mud. I will now contribute our own observations in this matter. One winter's morning we were sitting in bed clutching our tea cups when we saw a small black shape moving very quickly up the slope. It was moving so swiftly and smoothly that I at first thought that it was one of the crows flying up the hill just above the bracken level but there was something not quite right about the movement. So I turned aside to reach for my glasses, during which time the creature disappeared over the brow of the hill. Alan had been watching continuously and said that as it reached the top of the hill so it turned to run parallel to the house, and it appeared to be a very long cat, mainly black in colour but with grey stripes around the body. He reckoned that when we had first seen it running up the hill we were viewing it at a fore-shortened angle which made us think it was small and all-black. We have no opinions to offer. We just don't know what it was.

The wild beasts we see most of from the bedroom window are the frolicking grey squirrels which are not considered to be particularly malevolent except, possibly, by Foresters concerned about their young trees and some earnest people concerned about the decline of the red squirrel. However, other earnest people who reckon to know about these things consider that the red squirrel has declined through disease and that grey squirrels have simply moved in to take over the territories. But as we understand (from a well-informed friend) that it is the sturdy grey squirrel who is the healthy carrier of the very disease that kills the more vulnerable red squirrel, perhaps a controlled slaughter of grey squirrels in some places is justified.

There are no red squirrels in the Forest of Dean, so far as we are aware, so the grey squirrels have it all to themselves. They seem to have no predators (apart from the Forester with a gun) but this situation may change if plans go ahead for the introduction of the pine marten to these woodlands. We have read that the pine marten is a persistent enemy of squirrels and a female pine marten will kill a female squirrel in order to take over her nest. But as the pine marten also kills birds and steals eggs, its arrival in our woodlands won't do the already diminishing bird population any good at all. We feel uneasy about such an introduction, especially as we quite enjoy watching the grey squirrels. They chase each other in a follow-my‹leader scurry around the trees; they streak up the trunks and then seem to fly from tree top to tree top, alighting fleetingly on the slenderest of branches. We understand that these chasing activities are all part of the courtship performance, but I once watched a solitary squirrel fooling about in a most extraordinary way at the base of The Oak. He seemed to be grabbing up loose leaves and twigs, throwing them into the air and then somersaulting. Every now and then he would scrabble up the tree trunk for a few feet, then fall to the ground and repeat the somersaulting activity, occasionally running around the tree base in the meantime. Was he mad? Was he practising a courtship ritual? Or was he just full of the joys of being alive? To us the squirrels are entertaining little creatures and we hope that robbing birds' nests of eggs (as suspected in the case of our robins in the box) is an unusual activity indulged in by individual squirrels with depraved tastes.

The one place where grey squirrels can frolick without being a particular nuisance is in city parks and gardens. The same applies to that other charming countryside pest—the fox. Suburban foxes are sleek, well fed and welcome in most gardens. They may dig up a newly planted shrub if you have put bonemeal underneath it, and we have known a fox develop a taste for Jerusalem artichokes, but they can be such engaging creatures they are forgiven everything. Some warm-hearted people put out dog food at night for them and don't mind in the least if the fox decides to set up home underneath a garden shed. When we were living in a city suburb we were visited frequently by a saucy vixen who loved playing tricks on us. When Alan once left his garden shoes on the back doorstep he came out to find one missing and the vixen (we called her Freda) was trotting away with it in her mouth. We were able to retrieve it later from behind a neighbour's shed. She also stole one of Alan's leather gardening gloves, which she buried in the garden, and she sometimes dug up whole clumps of artichokes which she carried to another part of the garden to bury. Astonishingly, when she buried things in the garden she managed to rearrange the soil so cleverly that we only discovered her hoards by accident. She once charmed us into providing her with an instant meal. We were standing together at the back door when Freda trotted up and did a little dance in front of us. She went through a chasing-of-tail routine and then crouched with her head on one side looking up at us. As we made no immediate response she performed another little dance, all the while gazing coquettishly at us. The ploy worked. I went indoors and cut a bone from our weekend joint of lamb and gave it to her.

The foxes in the Forest don't want anything to do with us. Sometimes at dusk we will see one sneaking up the lawn to gather any titbits that the birds may have left, or to have a drink at the pond, but it disappears quickly into the night, intent upon urgent fox business which, in these parts, means trying to work out how to get into a fowl run. Anyone who wishes to keep chickens and to allow them free range amongst the bracken of the woodland knows that they may be in danger of attack from a hungry daytime raiding fox. Even birds secured into their house at night may be seized if there is the slightest gap through which a fox can wriggle. We like to hear that wild haunting cry of the vixen in the forest at night; but the man who has a fowl house of birds to protect is not so charmed. He will be reaching for his gun. A fox in a chicken house will kill as many birds as it can, but we do not believe that its motives are frivolous. The fox doesn't want to leave behind good food and, left to its own devices, it would return to take away and bury those birds that it had been unable to carry off initially. A local villager who lost several free-ranging birds in one afternoon found one corpse half-buried on the hillside. Freda, the tame suburban vixen, may fool around burying old gloves just for fun but that Forest fox wasn't joking. It was probably thinking of the hungry litter of cubs hidden away underground and waiting for food to be brought.

The animals that live in the Forest around us are usually seen only at a distance and fleetingly. But some of the very small ones come and live close by us, although the one that ended up in our bath didn't really mean to be *that* close. It was early one frosty December morning when I found it. I had gone into the bathroom, only half awake, and was astonished to see a small dark shape bunched up in the bottom of the bath. Even without my glasses on I could see that it was a pipistrelle bat. I assumed that it had crawled through a hole that was high up in the brickwork of the house in order to hibernate within the cavity wall. This hole (which we suppose had at one time accommodated an overflow pipe from a roof tank) is in the wall that carries the flue from the stove. So perhaps it had become too warm for the bat and during its wanderings around the cavity to find somewhere cooler it had crawled through another plumbing hole and had ended up in our bathroom. Our bathroom contains your usual sort of 'modern' ivory-coloured bathroom fitments and tiles and, as bathrooms go it is adequate. This was the bathroom we had taken over with the house and we had no intention of changing it, but to a little bat who likes dark and rough places it must have been a nightmare. I could imagine him flying wildly from one smooth bright wall to another, desperately trying to find a way out and finally ending up exhausted in the bottom of the bath. He must have died in torment. Except that he wasn't dead. I had called Alan to the bathroom and he bent over the bath and picked up the bat who immediately wriggled and gave a little squeak of protest. Standing there in our pyjamas we looked at each other and tried to remember what we knew about bats. Alan remembered from his childhood that a bat seeking hibernation quarters had been quite happy to cling to his bedroom curtains, and I thought I had read somewhere that a bat disturbed in hibernation would need a drink of watered‹down milk.

We knew that bats often liked places that were cold, dark, dirty and hanging with cobwebs, so we reckoned that the bedroom on the south-east corner of the house was the best temporary resting place for the bat, who had now been given the name of Pippy. The curtains in this room were of a dark brown coarse fabric. We partially drew them, to darken the room, and bunched up one of them upon the window ledge. I went to fill a shallow jar lid with a milk and water mixture whilst Alan gently eased Pippy from his hand onto the crumpled-up curtain. We then went downstairs to have breakfast and consult our bat book in order to decide what to do next.

In this book (*The Secret World of Bats* by John and Molly Hines) full instructions are given on the making of a satisfactory bat box. John Hines' bat box is obviously ideal for roosting and hibernating bats, but a group of bats would normally huddle together in such a box. We thought that Pippy, all on his own, might be too cold. Perhaps we should put him up in the roof? But we weren't altogether sure that, come the spring, he could find a way out.

In the event Pippy solved the problem for us. When we went up to the bedroom a couple of hours later we found that he had disappeared. We had left the bedroom window slightly open, but as it was then broad daylight we didn't think that Pippy would have ventured outside. We examined the curtains carefully but no bat was clinging anywhere in them. Looking around that room I realised that we, if not Pippy, had a problem. A walk-in cupboard (filled with hanging clothes) had been left with its door open. Clothes hung from the back of the room door. Open boxes of fabric, clothes, magazines and general junk were stacked on the floor and on top of a wardrobe. There were many places in that room where a tiny little bat could creep into and hide. This wouldn't have mattered except for the fact that the clothes were in frequent use and the boxes often riffled through.

For the rest of that winter I was extremely cautious on those occasions when I was obliged to interfere with anything in that bedroom. We considered that the cupboard would be the most likely spot chosen by Pippy and that dark jackets hanging there might seem inviting to a bat looking for somewhere to cling. So each time I took a jacket from that cupboard I examined it cautiously before putting it on. This was easy enough to do except for the sleeves. Even with a torch it is impossible to see clearly up, or down, a sleeve. In fact there is only one way to find out if you have a bat in your sleeve. You put your arm into it.

But we didn't find Pippy. I suppose it is possible that he spent an undisturbed hibernation somewhere in that bedroom and that he subsequently took himself off through the open window. We like to think so. And when we see the pipistrelle bats zippering around the house in the half dark at the end of a summer's day we like to pretend that Pippy is there amongst them.

It is very pleasant to live surrounded by small animals but we prefer them to keep to their normal habitat and to stay clear of ours. So when I noticed a busy little fieldmouse setting up home about two yards from the back kitchen door I decided that she must be discouraged. We have read that fieldmice do not normally come into the house but as they have several litters a year, and there could be nine babies in each litter, I wasn't taking any chances. Nosy young fieldmice might find our back kitchen an interesting place to explore.

I first noticed Mrs Fieldmouse when I was gazing out of the kitchen window and saw a movement on the path by the back door. It was a long-tailed fieldmouse carrying a dead oak leaf. She scuttled across a border containing chive plants and then disappeared into a small wall of loose stones we had built up around an old Belfast sink which was now filled with earth and growing winter savory. As I watched, so the fieldmouse reappeared and ran across the path towards the house wall and out of my sight. She soon came back again, carrying another oak leaf. I remembered that a lot of oak leaves had gathered beneath the timber stack at the back of the house, and it would seem that this was the bedding material she was after. All the time that I was watching her run to and fro I noticed that she followed the same route each time: across the chive bed and into the base of the stone pile. If I upset her routine perhaps she would be put off and go elsewhere. So I went out and removed the particular stones she always ran between, and I came back inside to watch. The fieldmouse seemed not to notice the missing stones. She continued carrying oak leaves into the stone pile, disappearing between stones in approximately the same position as before. Drastic action was called for. I removed all the stones from that side of the Belfast sink. I then saw what she was up to. Her little run finished up underground beneath the sink itself. But surely, now that her access point was entirely exposed, she would give up? Not a bit of it. She had set her heart on a nest beneath the Belfast sink and she carried more and more oak leaves into the little hole in the earth at the side of the sink.

Then I had a brilliant idea. I know that in daylight the field mouse is somewhat short-sighted. (I was once able to feed one by hand. It was unable to discern me squatting beside its run, but it could certainly smell the bit of cheese I was holding out. It put its two paws upon my finger and thumb and nibbled away happily at the cheese.) If I was prepared to wait patiently with a bit of cheese then perhaps I could catch this fieldmouse and take her down to the rough. On the other hand, I reckoned that a fieldmouse of such determination would soon find her way back to the half-completed nest beneath the Belfast sink. Somehow I had to put her off the whole idea of nesting there.

Perhaps, if an animal's eyesight is poor then its other senses are particularly acute, and sensitive. I went and fetched a large loud and clanging alarm clock and set it going right alongside her hole. Not only did this clock have a particularly aggressive tick, it had a repeater alarm of such deafening penetration that even from inside the kitchen I could hear the thing going off. Throughout the day I kept re-setting the alarm. I could imagine Mrs Fieldmouse sitting underground upon her neat pile of oak leaves, with her paws over her ears. She gave up. Even the most determined and long-suffering fieldmouse has her limits of endurance, and that alarm clock was beyond hers. We never saw her again. I placed a small stone across the entrance hole to her underground nest and this stone remained undisturbed. So the cosy underground home had been abandoned.

Whilst wishing to discourage such small rodents from entering the house we have no objection to them living in the garden, even though it is alleged that they do a lot of damage to growing crops. We have known them to be described as 'the despair of gardeners' but this has not been our experience at all. We suspect that a few crocus corm losses could be attributed to them, and any pea pods that actually dangle to the ground are sometimes nibbled but apart from this they have caused no damage that we have been aware of. We are equally happy to have field voles living in the garden, although they too have a reputation for destroying crops. The area of rough ground around our oak trees is obviously ideal field vole habitat but we can only assume that their numbers are kept under control by prowling foxes and stoats or hunting owls, because we have not found many of them.

I once came eye to eye with a field vole who had taken up temporary residence in a length of that afore-mentioned white painted guttering downpipe, which had been lying on the ground behind the buddleia bushes for so long that rank grass had enveloped it. As field voles make long runs above ground but hidden under long matted grass, this particular vole must have been very pleased at discovering this ready-made watertight tunnel which would successfully protect him from marauding foxes and owls if nothing else. How was he to know that one day I would come along and disentangle the downpipe from the grass? He probably felt quite safe sitting inside whilst he heard me blundering around in the grass, but when I lifted the pipe and up-ended it he suddenly found himself catapulted from his shiny tunnel and deposited on the grass at my feet. With his four feet splayed wide he just lay there and stared up at me in terror. I expected him to scuttle away but he didn't. He seemed to be petrified with fright. I crouched beside him. He appeared uninjured but he didn't take his eyes from my face. He just sat there, obviously waiting for death. With finger and thumb I picked him up by the scruff of the neck, looked into those terrified eyes, apologised for disturbing him, and placed him in an area of long grass out of the way. For a while he didn't move and I wondered if in fact he had died of fright, but when I looked a few minutes later he had gone.

Our stand of Jerusalem artichokes was, at that time, right at the edge of our vegetable garden and not far from that area of rough ground where I had disturbed the field vole. When in the following winter we saw a couple of little round holes about $1^{1}/_{4}$ins. in diameter entering the soil alongside one of the clumps we assumed that the field vole was showing his gratitude by stealing our tubers. But we were wrong. When we started to lift the artichokes we found none of them nibbled and none seemed to be missing. The only damage to that crop was caused by slugs, some of whom were still curled up inside the cavities they had made.

Which brings me to another point. Whilst the long-tailed field-mouse and the field vole are condemned for being the gardener's enemy (which hasn't been our experience) the noble toad and frog are exalted as being the gardener's friend (which hasn't been our experience either). We may, of course, be mistaken. We are delighted to have frogs and toads in the garden (and Alan has made special provision for their comfort amongst the stones and slabs) but they don't seem to be very efficient at doing what we would like them to do: eat the slugs, woodlice and other nasties. Perhaps if we didn't have our friendly community of frogs and toads the slug population in the garden would be much higher, but this is hard to believe. We have the huge long ones (both the handsome black variety and the repulsive orange-edged brown ones) but we think that they probably do less damage to our crops than those sneaky little grey or black ones that live in the soil and are not often to be found on the surface. As the toad spends most of its time underground too, what the hell is it doing down there—dozing? In fairness to the toad I must admit that in our book on toads, slugs are not listed as being a favourite part of its menu. But it is supposed to like ants (and we have enough of them to keep a colony of toads happy), and snails. Now, strangely enough, we don't have many snails. Has toad eaten them all? There are obviously a lot of mysterious things going on underground that we don't understand.

The toad's inclination to spend a lot of time in the ground rather than on it puts him at risk of being clobbered by the spade of an energetic gardener. Alan has on several occasions lifted to the surface a surprised toad upon his spade. By sheer chance he has never actually sliced a toad in two, and it sometimes worries him that this disaster could so easily happen. He has also been surprised at some of the narrow crevices into which a toad can squeeze. When once removing a paving slab from the top of another he half dragged the top slab aside to find underneath a flattened out but undamaged toad which had somehow managed to fit itself in between the two slabs. Alan has made a toad hole—or should it be Toad Hall?—in the rockery at the side of the pond and any toad found in the way of his gardening work is introduced to this hole. Each toad, so far, has dutifully clambered into the hole but they usually turn round inside the tunnel and sit looking out, no doubt waiting for Alan to get out of the way so that they can carry on being not particularly useful in the vegetable plot.

We have read that slow worms enjoy eating small slugs and we are sorry that so far we have not seen many slow worms here; to be precise, only one half-dead one and one tiny baby one. But our garden would appear to be a suitable habitat for them so we hope they will increase. Lizards too are not very numerous in this patch. We sometimes see them sunning themselves on top of a pile of junk in the rough, and on one occasion a lizard escaped from a hole in the house wall that Alan was about to fill up. It disappeared beneath a pile of junk near the house. As we understand that lizards eat ants, ant eggs and caterpillars, we are happy to continue providing them with piles of junk for their accommodation, which would seem to be much better living quarters for them than the cavity wall of our house.

Another slug eater we are delighted to have in the garden is, of course, the hedgehog. I don't think we have any living here, but they visit from time to time, quite often to drink at the pond. It's usually a solitary hedgehog we see bumbling about between the garden plants but on one occasion there were two adults out on the lawn at dusk and it was obviously Him and Her. She just wanted a drink at the pond. But he had other ideas. She clambered up onto the pond-side border, with him in close pursuit. She turned around and faced him and they had a nose to nose grunting discussion. She then walked away towards the water and he came up behind her. Again she faced him; again he tried to get around to her backside. Now this was interesting. Mating between two hedgehogs must be a difficult if not actually painful performance. So I continued watching. As she was obviously not going to be allowed to have a peaceful drink she gave up the idea and continued facing him. He tried to walk around her but she wasn't having it. She backed away. He was now grunting in exasperation but she continued walking backwards until she suddenly fell off the edge of the pondside rockery and landed in a heap on the lawn. He went after her. But now, in the gathering gloom, they were out of my sight behind the rockery stones. So I left them to it. Anyway, it seems that in the end he triumphed. About three months later a hedgehog came trundling up the lawn with a little prickly bundle running along beside it. I waited to see if baby hedgehog was going to be taught How to Drink at the Pond without Actually Falling In, but they turned aside and went nosing about amongst the broccoli plants. I don't know where baby's brothers and sisters were—we understand that hedgehogs usually have between three and seven young—but the whole family is welcome to spend as much time as it likes in our garden.

This invitation to our garden does not extend to that most ubiquitous Forest of Dean animal, the wandering sheep. After all, they should have everything they want out there in the woodland and along the tracks and roads. They nibble at the grass, wild thyme, violets, wood sorrel and young bracken. They push through the brambles, reach up to browse on overhanging young leaves of trees and in winter, when times get hard, a nice chap will come in a truck and bring them hay or other tempting sheep food. The same nice chap will bring food out to them when they are pregnant and need that little extra something to keep them going. This life of freedom (with back-up support) is taken for granted by the sheep because they claim they have ancient rights in this countryside. For hundreds of years they have been roaming the Forest tracks and roadside edges. They munch their way in and about the lanes, along the village street, and right through your garden if you leave the gate open. Little groups of them move around together, stopping every now and then, seemingly to consult each other about the next place to visit. 'Shall we do the woodland walk and see if the nettles are worth eating, or shall we investigate the cedar hedge behind the village hall?' Unfortunately these discussions often take place in the middle of the road, and whilst most motorists patiently wait for a decision to be made, some do not. Injury or death is the price some sheep pay for the freedom to roam. This is one of the reasons why an increasing number of local people are protesting that the time has come for this tradition to end. A wandering band of sheep will, of course, keep the roadside verges trim and neat with no expense to the local council, but when the wandering sheep move on they leave their droppings behind. This is another reason why many local people wish to see an end to the traditional rights of the sheep.

The men who own these wandering sheep are known, in local parlance, as 'sheep badgers' and they belong to a Commoners' Association through which they defend their rights to run sheep in the Forest. The Association claims that ancient laws granted these rights but the Forestry Commission has always argued that no such laws exist. However, in 1981 an agreement was reached between the Forestry Commission and the Commoners' Association whereby the grazing of sheep in the Forest was permitted, subject to certain conditions and outside of certain enclosed areas. The purpose of this agreement, so far as the Commission was concerned was, hopefully, to regulate the roaming of sheep and control their numbers. So, for the time being, the sheep are still wandering about in the lanes, woodlands and villages of the Forest of Dean.

Alan and I don't feel strongly about the dirt the sheep leave behind them. After living in suburbia, where piles of stinking dog mess are a normal hazard of pavement walking, we are not troubled by the comparatively dry sheep droppings that can be kicked aside if not avoided altogether. But then, we are fortunate in that the sheep don't choose to come and lie outside our house, and it is this aspect of their behaviour that causes problems. A small flock of wandering sheep will normally keep to a certain vague territory, defined entirely at the flock's whim, and when the time comes for a rest in order to chew, digest, snooze in the sun or shelter from the wind and rain, the flock will lie together against a bank or wall or fence. It is always the *same* bank, wall or fence. They will move off if you march up and say unkind things to them but they will not go very far away and will stand looking at you, just waiting for you to push off in order that they can return to their chosen resting spot. Day after day, month after month, year after year, the sheep will always return to the same bit of roadside for their afternoon snooze. They wear away the vegetation and they leave behind piles of droppings. When a group of them lie there together in the afternoon sunshine they may look charming to the person driving past, but the person living nearby knows that they don't smell very charming.

One of their favourite resting places is on the grass verge beside the church lychgate. In springtime it is a truly biblical scene—this flock of sheep with their lambs, slumbering against the old grey stone wall. If the daffodils and snowdrops are gracing the churchyard who can remain unmoved by this tranquil scene with its symbols of hope and rebirth? It is a sight to gladden your eye and uplift your heart—even if you do have to mind where you put your feet.

Of more concern to Alan and me is the risks the sheep run when wandering along the verges of busy roads. In early spring each ewe will be accompanied by one or two lambs. We know that when mother, in her offhand feckless way, decides suddenly to cross the road she will be followed by her tiny newly-born offspring on long trembling legs. We sometimes see family parties of sheep grazing at the roadside within inches of the fast-moving traffic hurtling past them. What might happen doesn't bear thinking about. So we stop thinking, and drive on. If the sheep were rounded up and spent their short lives cared for behind hedges in fields they would be much safer, if somewhat bored. And what would be the long-term effects within the Forest? It is interesting to speculate what might happen if the roadside verges and woodland plants were left to grow unchecked. Certainly it is noticeable what a profusion of wild flowers there are in those parts of Gloucestershire not far from the Forest where the sheep are not allowed to roam freely in the lanes.

Nevertheless, for the present, the sheep still have their rights here. Their voices are part of the background to our lives. The distant murmur of a flock, the worried bleat of a lamb and the reassuring answer of its mother—we would miss them if they weren't there. We would also miss those frolicking springtime lambs that chase each other around the trees and race through the dead bracken. We enjoy watching them enjoying themselves, even though we know that a large number of them will eventually end their lives at the Cinderford slaughterhouse.

Coming to terms with eating meat is something we had no problems with in the days long ago when we thought that most farm animals were treated with kindness and lived comparatively normal lives. But the revelations over the last ten to fifteen years of disgusting modern farming practices has caused us to eat less meat less often until we arrived at the present situation where we are almost non meat-eaters. Almost, but not quite. The animals that are killed to provide us with our occasional meals of meat were born and reared locally and didn't have to travel very far to be slaughtered. If I can buy a leg of lamb with the Forest of Dean mark stamped on it then I know that this animal has spent most of its life wandering in the Forest, selecting luscious titbits of grass, flowers, young bracken, nettles and occasional bits of overhanging trees—just as it fancied. In fact it might even be one of the little nuisances that chose to spend a lot of the time chewing at our *laurustinus,* pyracantha, cotoneaster bushes and anything else it could reach by clambering up onto our fence with its forefeet or pushing its nose through the palings. When we notice these capers we chase the lamb off. But, more often than not, it will just stand a few feet away, staring insolently, until we go indoors when it will return to the attack upon our hedge. I shall eat that leg of lamb with a clear conscience.

CHAPTER 13

Keeping the Home Fires Burning

One of the benefits of living in the middle of a Forestry Commission woodland is that we are granted the right to gather brushwood. Normally one has to pay £5 a year for this privilege but, as old age pensioners, we get it without payment. Whether this is a tacit acknowledgement of the impecunious state of many of us, or whether the Commission just considers that we are all too feeble to drag home much wood, I don't know. But, whatever the reason, we are grateful for the concession and we make full use of it. Our walks are never without purpose. When going out to see if the bluebells are in flower or to listen for the arrival of the willow warbler, we are also looking out for any suitable branches which might be lying around and which we can pick up on our way back.

> Oak logs will warm you well, if they're old and dry
> Larch logs of pinewood smell, but the sparks will fly

Anyone who burns wood on an open fire knows that these old sayings make sense. Unfortunately, under the terms of our Permit to Gather Brushwood any oak logs we drag home from the forest are likely to be old, wet and rotten. The Forestry Commission lays down strict rules for us wood gatherers. We are allowed to remove dead wood only, and it must measure less than 3ins. in diameter. No cutting tools must be taken into the forest and no timber lying around that has been sawn or axed must be gathered. Those haphazard branches that the Forestry Commission workers have chucked aside are forbidden to us. Well now, I never take a tape measure into the Forest with me and, as for those lovely smooth branches of birch and beech I drag home, how am I to know how those nice clean ends were cut? Was it saw or axe, or could it have been a brush hook? I am prepared to discuss the matter with the first Forestry Official who challenges me in the Forest. But I have never met a Forestry Official when I have been out gathering wood. Come to think of it, I have never met *anyone* when I have been out gathering wood. There has been no-one to see me searching amongst the bracken and undergrowth, and assembling my boughs in a neat pile to be looped around with a rope. I am observed only by the long-tailed tits, the goldcrests and an occasional curious robin. A jay may screech at me bad-temperedly. He probably thinks I am making too much noise. At home, in the sitting room, there is a watercolour hanging on the wall over my desk. It is a picture painted by the Victorian artist John Steeple and it depicts an old crone returning to her cottage with what appears to be a large bundle of brushwood upon her back. I often wonder why she didn't use a rope. It's much easier. Moreover, I find that if I am coming down a steep slope the long bundle dragging behind me acts as a very useful brake. So far, the Forestry Commission hasn't forbidden this practice.

> Birch logs will burn too fast, alder scarce at all
> Chestnut logs are good to last, if cut in the Fall

We don't have to travel very far to pick up kindling. We can find all we need in the garden. Our four oak trees are continually scattering twigs which are crisp, arthritically bent and sometimes still have dry autumn leaves clinging to them. These twigs are often covered with an attractive lichen-like growth called oak moss. Blueygreen flakes of this moss cling to the twigs, and these flakes sometimes form into little balls of feathery clusters. It all looks so pretty it seems a shame to burn them, but onto the fire they go where they catch alight with crackling enthusiasm and a scent of autumn woodlands. Trimmings from the cedar hedge, although green and limp, will flare and sizzle like firework 'sparklers' and add a fruity smell of pine to the room.

All woody trimmings from the garden are examined thoughtfully. Will this make good kindling or should it be added to the garden bonfire? Some of the best kindling comes from our stand of Jerusalem artichokes. The tall stems, some of them 2ins. in diameter, stay on the plants until the crop is lifted in winter, by which time they are crisp and hollow and look a bit like bamboo. But they are easy to snap by hand and are quick to catch alight. We keep a large kindling box in one of the sheds and the general idea is that all kindling is gathered on dry days and chucked into the box to stay dry. But we have never yet owned a shed that keeps everything dry, and the kindling brought into the house is usually damp. I once thought it would be a good idea to dry out a box of kindling overnight on the rack above the Aga. I didn't repeat this idea. Certainly the twiggery dried out well, but I wasn't very happy at the sight of woodlice and earwig corpses on the cooker top next morning. So we now have an evening routine of arranging a handful of kindling for tomorrow's fire in the hearth before we go to bed. Hemmed in by the fire guard it dries out quite safely, and any wildlife inadvertently carried in presumably takes itself off somewhere else. I have found no corpses in the hearth.

The burning quality of newspapers varies a lot and I find that *The Telegraph* is the best for starting the fire. Its pages, crisp and thin, make an excellent blaze. But the other broadsheets are useful for wrapping up parcels of damp small coal. A shovelful of coal dust tightly wrapped in *The Times* will make an excellent 'backlog', so long as the fire is well established and burning brightly at the front. I always make a point of reading the newspaper before it is burnt, but Alan doesn't usually bother. He will read any article of natural history, archaeological or scientific interest that I draw to his attention, but he passes over the rest. That is another of the benefits of being an old age pensioner and living in the middle of a forest. You can, to a large extent, ignore what's happening in the world outside.

> Ash logs are queen of all, burn them wet or dry
> But burn the elder not at all, or your luck will fly

I drag back from the Forest anything that looks burnable and in this way I have come to know what's good for the fire and what isn't. Elder certainly isn't. An elder tree planted in the garden may well protect you against lightning, thunderbolt, curses, maledictions and any other evil a passing witch may wish upon you, but it is almost impossible to get it to burn. Gypsies (according to what I have read) consider the elder to be sacred and would never burn it upon their fires. But I think the truth is that they *couldn't* burn it upon their fires. The twigs would just blacken, smoke, and go out. You try it (if you are prepared to risk the wrath of the Dark Powers) and see what I mean. But we would not dream of trying to burn elder. We are very fond of this tree and have encouraged it to grow wherever we live. There was no elder on this patch when we came, but we soon got one going and any twiggery cut from it is stuck into the ground in the hopes that another elder tree is forthcoming. It often is. (And I can assure you that we haven't seen a witch in years.)

I wish I had come across an old country saying that warned me about sumac; I might have been saved a lot of work. We once had to cut back a rather obstreperous sumac tree and the large boughs, sawn into 8ins. lengths (of about 4ins. diameter) looked ideal for the sitting room fire. They weren't. Even after being dried out in the sun all summer they burned with reluctance and sullen smokiness. What's more, they exuded a sticky resinous mess that dripped down the grate front. So, in the interests of posterity, I add my own Old Country Saying:

> Burn the sumac if you durst;
> from the Gods you'll get no quibbles
> But you may feel that you've been cursed,
> As the damn stuff smokes and dribbles

You will have noticed that, on the whole, gathering winter fuel is women's work in this household. Sawing it up is too. I persuaded Alan to make me a special saw horse, to my precise requirements. You know what a saw horse looks like—six hefty cross pieces of timber forming the legs and log guide, with a linking piece of hefty timber to support the log—and you often see them drawn in sketches illustrating 'The Countryside in Autumn' articles. There will be a cottage in the background with smoking chimney, a pile of swept autumn leaves and a man bent over a saw horse in the foreground, with a pile of uncut boughs to his left and a tumbling pile of logs to his right as they have fallen off the end of his saw horse. Well, that's the sort of thing I wanted, but it had to be a lot lower. That man bent over his saw horse obviously had strong shoulders and he was able to lean at a slight angle over his work. If I tried that I should be clutching my back in agony and would have to take to my bed for a week. But, if my back is a bit feeble my legs are not and I reckoned that if the saw horse was low enough for me to put one foot upon it, not only would my back be supported but my foot could help hold the log in position. My theory was right. With the saw horse Alan made me, my foot holds the log in place so securely that I can often get two hands on the saw. After an hour's work at my saw horse on a frosty winter's afternoon I come in to the kitchen red-faced, panting, demanding a cup of tea, and enjoying that general feeling of well being that comes after a period of energetic exertion in the cold fresh air.

We cannot drag home enough timber to keep us in fuel all winter, so we buy coal which is dug from the earth only a few miles away. Our coalman is one of the few remaining Free Miners. He digs the coal by hand each morning from his seams beneath the Forest floor and he delivers it to his customers in the afternoons. He has chosen a hard way of life. As well as coping with the conditions undergound—he works with pick, shovel and what he describes as 'an old cutting machine'—he has to continually argue with various Authorities whose demands certainly seem to make his life more difficult. We read about these difficulties in the local free newspaper. We understand that Free Miners must now have 'planning permission'. Licences are required (and have to be paid for) and certain Health and Safety regulations must be observed. But the Forest of Dean Free Miners are an obsti-nate bunch of men. They have been arguing with The Authorities for the past 700 years; they are not likely to give up now.

The system under which a man could gain a right to dig his own coal dates back to the Middle Ages. The conditions of application have remained unchanged. A prospective Free Miner must be 21 years of age or over. He must have been born in the Hundred of St Briavels and he must have worked for at least a year and a day in a mine. Such a man could then apply for a grant of land (called a 'gale') which he could mine for himself. As the Forest was originally one of the king's hunting grounds, all Free Miners had to pay a royalty to the Crown on the amount of coal dug from the ground. This royalty was collected by a king's officer called the Gaveller. All down the ages the Free Miners have continued to pay up their royal-ties to whoever owned the Forest. But, all down the ages, life in the Forest has been constantly changing. Trees were always required for ship-building. Moreover, hard-up kings found they could raise capital by leasing large tracts of land to ironmasters and coalmasters.

A PATCH IN THE FOREST

There was big money to be made in the Forest. Little men who insisted on their right to dig holes in the ground were a nuisance. They still are to Authorities.

As the Forest of Dean is no longer 'Royal' there is no Gaveller to collect monies due to the Crown. However, there is a Forestry Commission official called a Deputy Gaveller who oversees the Free Miners' affairs. But for how much longer are we going to have a Forestry Commission? It has already been partitioned into several sections, each with separate responsibilities. Has this been done with a view to selling the Forest all together? No-one seems to have answers to these questions at the moment. But, whatever plans the government has for its forests, it is likely that little men digging up coal don't feature in them. Come to that, I don't suppose that sheep 'badgers' and peasants picking up sticks feature in those plans either. It's probably best not to dwell too long on what might happen to our forests in the future. Let's get back to the fireside.

The coal delivered to us is of excellent quality—large bright and shining lumps that burn with a clear flame and give out plenty of heat. The chimney is swept once a year, in the summer, and we also have a yearly routine of washing the fire irons and grate front and polishing the copper coal scuttle. Local friends whose open fire is their main source of heat need the chimney swept four times a year, but our main living room is the kitchen, with the stove providing all the heat. We don't usually light the sitting room fire until mid-afternoon. The soot from our chimney and ashes from the grate are kept for use in the garden. If we have been burning mainly coal then the ashes and cinders are used along the narrow paths between our vegetable crops. But when we have log fires the ashes are gathered with particular care and stored in a shed. They will be dug into the ground to nourish the crops.

Elm is slow but hazel's quick, apple logs smell sweetly
Cut the cherry when it's thick and strip the willow neatly

When settling down in front of the fire on a winter's evening I usually intend to do something useful or interesting—like knitting, mending clothes or reading a book. But as soon as my feet are upon the footstool I find myself gazing into the flames and my thoughts

136

wander dreamily. With, perhaps, some gentle music playing and a glass of whisky in hand, I am perfectly content to sit there doing absolutely nothing. Well, not quite *nothing* because I am a front-of-the-fire fiddler. I enjoy feeding the fire with logs, or giving a large lump of coal a sharp poke, delighting in the sudden leap of flames. As the evening draws on a decision has to be made. Do we put on another log, or do we go to bed? We are sometimes reluctant to leave the glowing embers, and if the fire looks particularly clear and hot I will go and get the loaf of bread, toasting fork and the butter and we settle down to a late night snack which we don't need but thoroughly enjoy. I can't really work out why bread toasted on an open fire is so much tastier than toast done in any other way. You have to keep fiddling with it, rearranging the slice on the fork so that all parts of both sides of the bread get an even toasting, but the result is a crisp slice of toast, with just a hint of softness in the middle. You must then spread it thickly with butter and get your teeth into it just as the butter starts to melt. Unfortunately it is so delicious it is absolutely necessary to have a second slice. We sit there eating dribblingly tasty hot buttered toast until the fire starts to die down. If you haven't ever eaten wholemeal bread toasted upon an open fire then you have missed out on one of life's gastronomic delights.

But fires that burn with welcoming brightness in the evening are cold, grey and cheerless the following morning, and I must admit that I am a bit sluggish when it comes to the chore of clearing out the ashes. Now my mother-in-law knew how to manage a fire. She attended to it with the diligence and competence that she applied to every household task. She belonged to that generation of respectable artisan-class women who strictly adhered to certain rules of conduct (like always having the doorstep well scrubbed, the brass polished, and keeping the privet hedge cut frequently so that no blossom appeared), and the tending of the fire followed an unwavering routine. She was up in the morning before first light and on her knees in front of the hearth. I remember that she kept a special sacking pinafore for the job, and her tools and gloves were in a tidy little basket. By 8 a.m. my mother-in-law, in a clean pinny, would be sitting beside a brightly burning fire. The hearth tiles would be shining; the grate bars, hobs and trivet, newly-polished with Zebo would be black and gleaming. There was no sign of dust anywhere.

She didn't think there was anything exceptional about her routines. This was normal housewifely practice in her way of life. Any woman who wasn't sitting beside her fire ready to receive visitors by 8 a.m. was obviously a feckless slut—which just about puts me in my place.

To start with, it's usually mid-morning before I get around to the job and, being in a hurry, the hearth doesn't really get the attention it needs. As I shovel up the ashes the dust will settle gently upon all surfaces in the room and I promise myself that I will do a bit of dusting after *tomorrow's* fire because I haven't really got time today. Like my mother-in-law I keep special tools and gloves for the job, but when reaching up the chimney with the brush I can rarely avoid a brief but filthy contact with the side of the flue. My mother-in-law managed things better. In all the years I knew her I never saw her with a sooty right elbow.

It is possible that I learned the 'waste-not-want-not' philosophy from her, but she would be surprised at some of the things we burn on our sittingroom fire. We occasionally re-cycle plastic bottles and old shoes by adding them to the blaze, but I must admit that the first time I heard about the combustible qualities of shoes I wondered if I was having my leg pulled. However, at the time of receiving this information my old gardening shoes had splits in the leather uppers and disintegrating welts so I decided to try disposing of them on the fire. Previously I had always laboriously cut up the leather bits of any old shoes and added them to the compost heap, but if they could be reduced to ash in the fire so much the better. These shoes had rubber soles and leather uppers so one evening I cautiously intro-duced them, one at a time, to the fire. The flames from the burning oak logs licked in an exploratory way around the first shoe and then, quite suddenly, seized upon it with an eager roar. Each shoe curled and buckled and finally disappeared almost entirely, leaving just a small metal plate and a pile of soft ash. I reckon we got twenty minutes of flames and warmth from the pair of them.

Beechwood fires burn bright and clear; hornbeam blazes too
(But for a fire that's hot and fierce, just try a worn-out shoe)

CHAPTER 14

Pleasures and Pastimes

We don't get many visitors, neither do we go visiting very often. People from outside the Forest, when visiting us for the first time, usually arrive late. Sometimes very late. They complain of misleading signposts and roads that 'went the wrong way'. Some of our visitors are a little uneasy in the Forest; they think it is an odd place.

There are plenty of places to visit in the Forest of Dean. There is the Dean Heritage Centre, Clearwell Caves, Puzzle Wood, Soudley Ponds, Cannop Ponds and the well-known Mallards Pike Pond. There are many 'nature trails' and near Speech House there is a 'Sculpture Trail'. One of these days we really must go and see some of these places but so far we haven't found the time. Yet when people ask us what we do with our time here we find it difficult to answer. The fact is that we spend a lot of time doing nothing.

A frequent doing-nothing time for us is just as the light fades on winter afternoons. We sit in the kitchen while the winter's gloom gathers around us. If we put on the light and draw the curtains we might miss something. At about five o'clock on one January afternoon a large and brilliant full moon crept up over the crest of the hill to the east of us. As it slowly climbed up into the sky behind the woodland it appeared to get tangled up in the naked branches of the trees. It was such as astonishingly large moon and it seemed so close that it was absolutely necessary to stand there and watch its progress through the tree tops. But at the same time the sun had just set in the south-west, leaving a brilliant sky of red, pink, mauve and yellow. All the trees were silhouetted against the glowing light—the sturdy crown of The Oak, the delicate tracery of the birch and the upright

139

twigs of an ash. In the background the Forest conifers formed a black frieze on the horizon. I wandered back and forth between the front window and the back window. I couldn't make up my mind which spectacle of light I should be looking at. As the exuberance of growth immediately around us obscures much of our horizon in summer, it is only in winter that we get these dramatic sunsets and we have to stand at the window and watch them. We often see the end-of-day flight of birds; sometimes a high-flying and beautifully organised flock of seagulls will fly southwards to the Severn Estuary; a skein of geese with outstretched necks, or a few ducks with rapid wing beats will head north east—presumably to their overnight roosts on one of the ponds. Only when darkness has fallen and there is nothing to see outside do we put on the lights and draw the curtains.

The sunlight plays some strange tricks in this valley. One winter's morning when we were sitting in bed drinking our tea we became aware of something magical but impossible happening to the woodland slope outside. It was bathed in a glow of muted sunshine. The wet trunks of the trees glistened, the old mossy hawthorn across the way was a warm, soft green colour and the bracken-covered slope was a gleaming bright chestnut. But it was impossible for the sun to be shining on this eastern slope. It hadn't yet risen high enough in the sky to touch even the top of The Oak, although it was lighting up the forest on the other side of the valley. We wandered from room to room looking out of the windows and up into the sky. Then we realised what was happening. Immediately over the house was a large bank of billowing white cloud. The rising sun was touching the cloud and its light was reflected back upon our stretch of woodland.

Perhaps it is in the autumn that the light in this valley is at its mysterious best, when the morning mist is gradually being dispersed by the rising sun. The mist will hover and cling around the trees, but then the great shafts of sunshine will fall in straight lines between the tree trunks and the mist rises in swirling drifts away from the woodland. The sun will alight on dying bracken fronds and wet twiggery and a lace network of spiders' webs is revealed. They loop from stem to leaf and across wide gaps, in single or multiple strands. All hedge tops in the garden are knitted with a shawl of silver glistening strands. But the moment doesn't last. As the sun climbs higher and the angle of light changes, so the glinting webs gradually disappear.

I have now spent three paragraphs waffling on about lighting effects, and I haven't yet mentioned the stars. Mind you, our view of the sky is somewhat limited, but on a clear night we can always pick out the north star and the most readily recognisable constellations, and we had some excellent sightings of the Hale-Bopp comet when it was with us. But the point I am trying to make with all these concerns of moonshine, sunlight and star gazing, is that you can perhaps now understand how we find it very easy to spend a lot of time doing nothing. And being able to do nothing without feeling guilty is yet another one of the benefits of being pensioners.

Having spent most of our working lives engaged in various forms of humble employment (in between periods of unemployment) the need to earn a living has always occupied a lot of our time, thoughts and energies. But we no longer have to work for money, and the sense of freedom is exhilarating. Each morning we awake to a day stretching ahead that can be filled with whatever activity we choose. To a large extent the weather influences our choice. So far as Alan is concerned the decision is straightforward. It is either an 'indoor' day or an 'outdoor' day, and he makes his plans accordingly. But I have known him go out into the garden expressing the intention of, say, digging over the marrow bed, but I later find him out there painting the shed. He says his plans are flexible. I say they are non-existent. I reckon the day just 'happens' to him, without any forethought being involved. Now *I* try to be more organised. I start by looking at the *Radio Times* and marking those programmes which either of us might wish to hear. I then plan the timing of coffee making, lunch and dinner preparations and I set aside little mundane indoor jobs for myself (ironing, mending, cupboard turning out) to coincide with, say, the broadcast of a play. But my plans don't always work out either. For example, I go out to hang up the washing then get side-tracked into sniffing the sweet rocket, yanking a few weeds out of the shallot bed or checking up on the gooseberry crop, and forget all about the talk on Travels in Tibet we were going to hear. We are always missing the last episodes of serial plays, and we sometimes catch just the tail end of a concert. Our *Radio Times* is full of circled items representing possibly interesting programmes that we didn't hear.

Fortunately our enjoyment of music doesn't have to rely upon today's radio broadcasts. We have a large collection of cassette tapes, assembled over the last twenty-five years, some of which recall happy memories of madrigals and light opera we have attended, but most of which are recorded radio broadcasts. These recordings date back to the days when the announcers on Radio 3 had pleasant voices, seemed to understand what they were talking about, and could pronounce the names of composers. Whatever music we are in the mood for—vespers or dances, solemn or merry, solo flute or full orchestra, choral singing or folk songs—Alan will find a suitable tape. An evening of music in front of the sitting room fire is one of our pleasures.

We didn't know, until we moved here, that there were other musical pleasures to be enjoyed in the Forest of Dean. Almost every village has its silver band. Moreover, if you gather together a few Foresters, they will sing. Now, in the past, neither Alan nor I was particularly interested in brass or silver bands or male voice choirs. We associated them only with mining areas of England and Wales and thought the sounds they made were sometimes mildly pleasant but uninspiring. Large scale commercial mining in the Forest of Dean ended during the 1950s, but the musical tradition lives on and the first time we heard a performance by a local village silver band we were astounded—by the obvious talent, the controlled musicality of the performance and the downright glorious noise they made. We were tremendously impressed with the enthusiasm and age range of the band—from very young girls to quite elderly gents. I became a camp follower of the band and would turn up at any local fête or jamboree where they were performing. We are also enthusiastic admirers of the Forest of Dean Male Voice Choir. To watch and hear them perform is almost spell-binding. Their singing can get my feet tapping and then, with the next song, I am struggling to control a lump in my throat. Sometimes the Forest of Dean Male Voice Choir will visit our village, and when they are putting on a performance in conjunction with a silver band then we know we are in for an evening of tremendous enjoyment. We set off from home with nothing in our pockets but a torch and a small amount of money. (The evening will normally cost us less than five pounds, and this often includes a glass of wine during the interval.) A few hours later we will trudge home through the woods after an evening of music that has been some-times inspiring, sometimes uplifting, and always full of joyful noise.

PLEASURES AND PASTIMES

Our local silver band has a seasonal tradition of making a Christmas Day perambulation of the village. I understand that the band was formed in 1893 and it has been playing at village carnivals, school fêtes and church services ever since. Such are the acoustics in this valley that when the band is making its Christmas Day tour we can always hear them coming long before they arrive here. Last Christmas Day the weather was clear and very cold, and at mid-morning we could hear the band giving an enthusiastic rendering of 'We Three Kings' outside the hotel. In the silence that followed we knew that the band was walking up through the woods, and we heard 'Hark the Herald Angels Sing' coming from the group of cottages at the end of the lane. Shortly after this they were playing 'In the Deep Midwinter' outside our door and then, having received our dona-tion, they trudged off with their instruments. The faint but cheerful notes of 'God Rest ye Merry Gentlemen' came to us from over the brow of the hill and then they were gone, leaving us to the frosty still-ness of the woods.

As we choose to spend most of our time at home it is extremely fortunate that so much musical enjoyment can be ours—either at home or within walking distance. The same applies to our other great pleasure—that of reading. Our personal library which lines the walls of the sitting room (and overlaps into kitchen and bedrooms), coupled with the visiting Forest of Dean mobile library provides us with reading material that will last us for ever. But that worries me slightly—the thought of all those thousands and thousands of books I am not going to read because I will run out of time.

I read everything: posters, timetables, soap packets, advertise-ments. Wherever there are two or three words gathered together I will read them. I occasionally enjoy browsing through magazines (especialy old ones) and we buy one broadsheet newspaper a week, but magazines and newspapers are of transient interest. For good, solid, non‹stop enjoyment it is necesary to have a book in your hands. When reading a book I become lost in a world that the author is creating. If the author makes a point that needs thinking about I can lay the book aside and think. If the book belongs to us it will be placed back in its position on the shelf and as the years go by it can be read over and over again when the urge comes to enter the world created by that particular author.

Most of our books are old and we bought them second hand. At the last reckoning we found we had about 750 in our library, most of them bought by Alan who has spent more time idling in second-hand bookshops than I have. Generally speaking I am very pleased with the books he has acquired (although I haven't much use for titles like *Timbers of North America*, *The use of Timber in Mining*, *Infra-red Photography*, or *Optics of the Telescope*), but it was many years before I did much more than flip through the pages of the books he brought home. This was because I looked upon our personal library as a literary hoard that should not be raided until times were hard and books unobtainable outside the home. I foresaw the time when the library system would collapse altogether, or that I would become too old and feeble to get to a library. Then would be the time to open the covers of the books patiently waiting for me upon the shelves at home. During all the years we lived in town I brought home armfuls of books from the public library every week or so, and the books Alan brought home from the second-hand book shops were (so far as I was concerned) reserved for later years. Those years have now arrived. It is not that the library system has collapsed altogether (well, not quite) or that I am now too feeble to get to a library, but that the excellent mobile library comes during the late afternoon every fortnight and stops half a mile away from us on the other side of The Tumps. The Tumps is an area of overgrown old mine workings, full of hills, dips and holes. There are excellent views over the forest from the top of The Tumps and a walk across them in summer is enjoyable. But finding my way across them by torchlight on a wet and stormy winter's afternoon, with a rucksack full of books on my back, is not so enjoyable so my attendance at the mobile library is a bit haphazard.

I should point out that we have no specialised knowledge of old books. There are no valuable first editions in our library. They are simply books whose subjects interest us or whose authors are known to us and loved by us. But we are very much aware that other people have owned these books. Other hands, some of them long dead, have turned the pages. For example, some years ago we bought from a market second-hand bookstall a copy of H.V. Morton's *In Search of Wales* (published in 1941) but I didn't get around to reading it properly until recently. The writer had arrived at Anglesey and as I turned over page 91 to follow his travels I was astounded to find a handwritten letter folded inside. 'My own darlingest' I read. I hesitated for a moment and then, feeling rather sneaky, I read on. H.V. Morton's journey was forgotten. The letter, dated 8th August 1942 was written by Eric stationed at 385 Battery, R.A. Orkney, to his wife Margaret, and recalled with tender details their marriage of the previous year and their honeymoon at Tenby. *In Search of Wales* was, wrote Eric, an inadequate wedding anniversary present but he could find nothing more suitable in the local town of Kirkwall. So what happened? Was Eric killed in action? Did Margaret die in the blitz? Or did the arrival of this book on a street market stall have a more mundane explanation? We shall probably never know. And the very private love letter has been replaced in Morton's *In Search of Wales*, where it belongs.

Our set of Thackeray's novels (leather bound, gold-leaf edged, published 1900) was first owned by Muriel Midgley who bought it 'with some Christmas money in 1901', according to the inscription in the front of each book. Presumably Muriel bought the complete set of Thackeray because she knew and loved his novels, but we notice that many of our books on topography and natural history were originally awarded as school prizes and may not have been particularly cherished. A.R. Hope-Moncrieff's book *The Peak Country* had been awarded as a 'holiday prize' in 1915 but no-one had read it all the way through. We could tell this because the book had been bound in the old-fashioned way and needed to be 'opened' by its first reader. We found several pages still joined at the edges and had to slit them open ourselves. (Books that have been 'opened' by hand are left with a noticeable deckle-edge to the pages.)

Practical books are bought for the useful information they contain. We have books on soft furnishing, hand-loom weaving and gardening—all over half a century old, all containing valuable information, and most of them purchased for less than 2s.6d. We paid only 1d. for Warne's *Everyday Cookery Book* edited by Mary Jewry (probably at the end of the 19th century, but the publishers give no date) and the information it contains is fascinating rather than useful. I can't see me needing the advice on 'How to prepare a croquet party for twenty persons'; I am unlikely to want to make milk and suet gruel for an invalid and I hope I don't ever need the instructions for removing bed pests with Hudson's Paraffin Soap. But I expect that this little book was kept handy in the kitchen of Miss Amy Browne of

45 Ashley Road, Bristol, who wrote her name and address inside the cover, and whose homely notes on bits of paper are scattered throughout the book. Amy has jotted down the cooking times for rabbit, pigeon and chicken; she scribbled out a recipe for fruit cake and made a few (sometimes inaccurate) £.s.d. calculations. I couldn't throw away Amy's bits of paper. They will stay where they have always been, inside her book.

Common Weeds of Farm and Garden (published by John Murray in 1910) has been a first-class identification book for us, but every time I pick up *Vegetable Growing* by Walter Brett (published 1943) I get side-tracked to the back cover where inside, on the last blank page, there is a pencilled draft letter. It is a very ordinary letter to 'Joyce' enquiring about a fur coat she has for sale because the writer would like to buy it for his wife Betty. There are lots of crossings out, which seems surprising as it is written in a very scholarly hand. One would have thought that such a person as this writer would have had no difficulty in getting his thoughts down on paper. So, almost every time I pick up the book to see what advice is offered on peas, leeks or cabbage, I find myself turning to the back cover and wondering afresh why the letter was scribbled there, and whether or not Betty got the fur coat.

When a much-loved and scruffy old bookshop closed down some years ago we spent some time rummaging in the cluttered corners and came away with an armful of books, including a delightful volume called *Field Flowers, A handy book for the Rambling Botanist* by Shirley Hibbard. Combining factual diagrams, poetry and coloured drawings, it is a month by month flower guide—made all the more charming by the pressed flowers between the pages. But there is no signature or date inside the book. We guess that it may have been published at the beginning of this century. We don't know who has owned the book since but, on a summer's day a long time ago, someone with careful hands picked a white campion, a mallow, two buttercups and a beech leaf and pressed them between the pages, and there they will stay.

We buy new books occasionally, but cautiously. They are mostly reference books but if we read an interesting book review, or hear an extract on the radio, I will try to order a copy from the mobile library and only if the book appears to be one we would read again and again will we buy a copy. But this caution is not extended to the extremely cheap paperback reprints of out-of-copyright classics. It astonishes me that, at the time of writing, you can pay nearly £3 for a magazine containing badly-written and inaccurate information, whereas for the same price you could buy three paperback 19th-century novels which will provide months of enjoyment for me (and to a lesser extent Alan). I don't know what this plethora of cheap reprints is doing to the book trade, but I know it's giving Alan a few problems. As fast as he puts up new shelves, I will fill them with books. I ask for more bookends (which he makes out of polished wood and metal to a crafty design of his own, which enables a line of books to be held securely with the weight of the end ones) but we are running out of level surfaces upon which to place them. One of these days we shall have to stop buying books. But not just yet.

Sometimes we are tempted away from home in pursuit of pleasure. Sometimes we may turn our backs on the flower borders that need weeding, the seedlings that need thinning, the grass that needs cutting and the fruit that needs picking. Sometimes I can say to hell with the dirty windows, the pile of washing up, the dusty sitting room and the unmade bed—we are going out. We pull on our boots, lock the front door behind us, and step out into the Forest.

Sometimes our walks are for a definite purpose: to see if the violets are in bloom, to look for bluebells, check up on the foxglove clearing, hunt for chestnuts or bring home some wood for the fire, but often we go walking simply because that is what we decided to do with the day. Sometimes we are out for just a couple of hours; sometimes it's much longer and I often find that when it comes to making a decision *where* we are going to walk our ideas differ. I prefer to make for the high ground where I can look out over the Forest stretching to the distance; where I can see the sky and watch the buzzard soaring overhead and maybe hear the muted 'kronk kronk' of a pair of high-flying ravens. Alan enjoys this too, but he also likes the secret watery places where a stream finds its way through the overhanging trees and there are interesting mosses, tiny flowers, furtive little creatures that rustle beneath the bracken or plop discreetly into the stream, and the small flitting birds will watch us silently. When we set out for a walk it is usually the intention (*my* intention) to make for the ridgeway, but we often end up crawling along a damp ditch.

A favourite walk of ours includes a visit to a public house which stands in isolation upon a knoll the other side of our particular bit of

Forest. We usually approach it along a broad track which has distant views, and we return from the pub along overgrown footpaths that skirt the Forestry Commission plantations and wind through open woodland glades. Sometimes the footpath disappears and at one stage it arrives at a junction of similar footpaths, all of which had us confused and blundering about the first time we went that way. (Note: We find the Ordnance Survey maps of limited use when walking in the Forest of Dean, particularly the new $2^1/_2$ins. to 1 mile 'tourist' one. With some details obscured by bright blue symbols indicating car parks and camp sites [and with bright blue telephone symbols— usually about a quarter of a mile from the actual kiosk] this map leaves out many of the footpaths which are still used, includes some that can no longer be traced and, in one bit of woodland, indicates and names a house which was pulled down half a century ago and which can now only be traced as a few stones underneath the brambles.)

When we return from a walk in the Forest the rest of the day will be spent doing nothing in particular. Alan will turn out a pocket full of leaf samples taken from plants he had noticed but didn't recognise. This will mean going through several reference books in an endeavour to identify them. The bird books will be consulted to see if we can find anything resembling, say, a particularly small and noisy bird that tantalisingly kept out of sight and flitted between the high branches overhead. Moths and occasional not‹seen-before butterflies will have to be looked up. (We saw our first marbled white butterfly last year. It was feeding on thistles beside a track across heathland.) I will potter about the kitchen preparing food and clearing up a bit, but not much else gets done that day.

Some days I decide, quite suddenly, to go for a walk by myself. Alan insists on knowing exactly where I plan to go—sometimes I even stick to the plan—and these walks are much quicker and shorter excursions. I am never away for longer than one or two hours, and I rarely see anyone else. One of those rare occasions ocurred last October when I stopped to gather chestnuts from a tree beside the track, which wasn't far from a road. This chestnut tree was one of a line standing beside a bend in the track and its branches were hanging very low over the undergrowth of bracken and bramble. Underneath this particular tree the ground was littered with fallen chestnuts so I squatted there picking them over and stuffing my pockets full. Something caused me to look up and I saw

148

approaching me along the track a middle-aged couple walking slowly. It occurred to me that dressed as I was in my usual green and mud-coloured attire it was quite possible that the man and woman would walk straight past without noticing me. On the other hand if they *did* see me squatting there they might think I was having a pee and we would all be embarrassed. I could, of course, just leap out onto the track and say something jolly like 'Isn't it a lovely day', or 'Aren't the chestnuts good this year', but they were now so close to me I would surely startle them. So I stayed put. And then I noticed the dog about 20 yards behind them coming along the track. The man and woman were now walking past me, oblivious of my presence, but surely the dog would sniff me out and raise an uncalled-for alarm. I was wrong; the dog, walking as slowly as the man and woman, ambled past me. Grey muzzled and overweight, he wasn't up to doing anything exciting like raising alarms. I waited until man, woman and dog were out of sight along the track and then I crawled out from the bushes and went home with my chestnuts.

I know that during Bank Holidays and on all weekends there are likely to be other people in the Forest but during the working week, particularly when the weather is dull, I usually have the place to myself. I once went out on a November afternoon when I walked further than I had planned and stayed out later than I should have. I was hoping to see some deer. As autumn is the rutting season I thought that perhaps they would be too occupied with passionate pursuits to notice me walking slowly and as quietly as possible. But I saw nothing; not even a squirrel. There were no sounds in the Forest. Nothing was stirring. No birds called. I saw just one sullen-looking blackbird that sat amongst a tangle of dead bramble and glared at me moodily as I went past. The woods were particularly dank and dark apart from a splash of light from a line of beech trees with their coppery leaves. The birch trees still had a tattered veil of tiny pale yellow leaves and there were a few bronze spears of leaf clinging to the chestnut trees, but they were just a fringe of light to the dark brooding gloom of the conifers beyond. It was bitterly cold. When my head and ears became too uncomfortable I was obliged to pull up my jacket hood even though there was no wind blowing.

There was no view over the Forest because the dark grey of the distant trees could hardly be distinguished from the lowering grey sky above. I decided I might as well go home, which was just as well because the afternoon was closing in and the light was quite definitely withdrawing from the woodlands. I took a short cut through a plantation where the Forestry men had been clearing. The thick ruts made by their machinery had churned up ridges that were now frozen solid and all the fallen branches were stuck firmly to the ground. A particular bough of silver birch took my fancy and I tried to prise it away from the earth but it didn't budge, so I gave it a good kick and managed to shift it. I didn't have my rope with me so I heaved up one end of the bough, held it beneath my arm and then stumbled off down the slope dragging my booty behind me.

I rejoined the main track which was now just a dim line of light between the stands of Douglas fir. My dragging bough, with its spread of small branches gouging into the loose surface, was making a lot of noise. It was an unseemly intrusion into the almost cathedral-like quiet of that glowering forest. Moreover, it was slowing me down. The bough was much too long to get onto my shoulder so I decided to abandon it. I dragged it to the side of the track and rolled it into the gorse bushes. I could return to pick it up tomorrow, I told myself. I then stepped out along the track. A mist was now forming between the trees but I was still able to see well enough to avoid the ice-rimmed muddy puddles. My boots crunched along amongst the loose stones. It brings on quite a lonely feeling when the only sound you can hear is the crunch crunch of your own footsteps. Then, in the distance, I heard the muffled striking of the parish church clock. Only four o'clock and yet it was almost dark. I was now striding out as fast I could, and wondering if I was going to get told off when I got in. As I came down the last stretch of track I could see our house, with the light streaming out from the kitchen window. I caught a whiff of wood smoke and knew that Alan had lit the sitting room fire. An owl flew on silent wings across the track in front me. A dog fox yapped in the distance. This was their Forest, not mine. It was time I was out of it.

When I opened the front door I smelt something delicious. Pikelets. Alan was obviously in the kitchen making pikelets on the Aga hotplate. Toasted pikelets in front of the fire. What an excellent idea. I shut the door against the fog and frost and sat down to take off my boots. I was home.

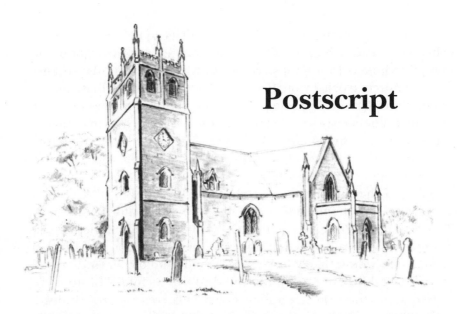

Postscript

The parish church is in the middle of woodland and was built at the beginning of the 19th century to serve a scattered community of small villages. A network of footpaths connects each village with the church and although one can imagine a pleasant stroll through blue-bell woodlands to Morning Service in springtime, it might have been a somewhat daunting experience for the Evensong worshippers on a stormy January night. Perhaps the church was built in the middle of the woods so that it was equally inconvenient to all villages; a sure way to forestall any complaints of undemocratic decision making by the Parish Council. However, a surfaced track now leads from one of the villages to the church and this is the route most car-owning parishioners use these days.

The church windows have no coloured glass in them and from inside you can see through them to the surrounding Forest, although with the age of the glass and the pattern of the leaded panes, the woodland outside is just a green blur. If the church door is left open you can sometimes hear the mew of a high flying buzzard, the calling of sheep and the soughing of the wind. The church stands upon a grassy knoll and there is always a slight wind moving around the buildings and between the gravestones. From the churchyard the view is over waves of trees, an area of heathland and, upon the far horizon, the uneven rooftops of a distant village.

A PATCH IN THE FOREST

The parish church is important to the villagers, believers and non-believers alike. Celebration of the traditional festivals throughout the year provides a background structure to village life, and the striking of the church clock throughout the day reminds us that time is passing, for all of us. For some people the church provides hope for the future. For everyone it is a link with the past. The surnames on the churchyard gravestones are still with us today, upon the electoral roll.

Living in the middle of the Forest and watching the yearly miracle of the changing seasons—the surge of new growth in the spring, the ripening of the summer crops, the aching loveliness of the autumn woodlands—it is impossible not to believe in a Creator. There must be some overall Power; some master planner behind all these cycles of growth, death and renewal. But is it the loving God of Christian belief, or is it more likely to be some remote unknown God; a God of pitiless indifference, to whom the death of a child is of no more consequence than the trampling down of a tree sapling? Indeed, such a God would be unaware of child and sapling. Both would be just part of a pattern of some overall scheme. No tidings of comfort and joy to be found here.

Whether it is a grand plan or an accidental pattern, Alan and I know that we are part of it. We trust that the sun will always rise in the morning behind the woodlands to the east of us, and will set each evening behind the distant Forest horizon in the west. But we will not always be here to see it. Now in the autumn of our lives we try to come to terms with our mortality. The day will come for each of us when we have to leave this patch of land and go and join the company of sleepers beneath the turf in that other little clearing in the Forest, beside the parish church. ....

But in the meantime there's work to be done. I think I will go and pick the sprouts for dinner.

Appendix

Bird List

Not all the birds that we see can be positively identified. Those flocks of high-flying gulls are probably either herring gulls or black-headed gulls. Alan reckons to be able to tell them apart, but I am never sure. And although we think the fast-flying ducks are probably shelduck or mallard, we have no idea what the geese might be. Then there are the mystery birds. We once watched four birds on the topmost branches of The Oak and we knew we hadn't seen such birds before. They seemed to be hammering at something; maybe acorns wedged in cracks or held beneath feet? They appeared to be about jackdaw size but with longer beaks. But we could see no colours on them at all. They were just dark shapes against the sky. Could they have been nutcrackers? Then there was the chough. I didn't see it but Alan did. There is no other crow with a curved orange beak and orange legs. This one flew across the garden, Alan says, followed by Jo in noisy pursuit. A chough has no right to be in the Forest of Dean. I query Alan's identification, but he has no doubts, and we are still arguing about it. But there is no argument about most of the birds we see around us. Here they are:

Birds visiting the garden: Blackbird, Blackcap, Brambling, Chaffinch, Chiffchaff, Crow (Carrion), Dove (Collared and Stock), Dunnock, Fieldfare, Flycatcher (Spotted), Goldfinch, Greenfinch, Jackdaw, Jay, Linnet, Magpie, Martin (House), Merlin, Nuthatch, Pheasant (female, once only), Pigeon (Wood), Redpoll, Redstart, Redwing, Robin, Siskin, Sparrowhawk, Sparrow (House and Tree), Starling, Thrush (Mistle & Song), Tit (Blue, Coal, Great, Long-tailed and Marsh or Willow),

Treecreeper, Wagtail (Blue-headed variant, Grey and Pied), Warbler (Garden and Willow), Whitethroat, Woodpecker (Green and Pied), Starling Wren, Yellowhammer (a pair, once only).

Birds seen flying over, or seen/heard in nearby woodland and heathland: Buzzard, Cuckoo, Goldcrest, Gull (Black-headed or Lesser Blackback), Hawfinch, Heron, Kestrel, Mallard, Moorhen, Nightjar, Owl (Tawny), Peregrine Falcon, Pipit (probably Meadow), Raven, Pheasant, Swallow, Swift.